Essentials of Reading & Writing English

A Basic English Literacy Program

Judith S. Rubenstein • Janet M. Gubbay

Printed on recyclable paper

NTC Business Books

a division of *NTC Publishing Group* • Lincolnwood, Illinois USA

To our husbands,
Howard S. Rubenstein and
Jacob D. Gubbay,
whose encouragement and support
made this possible

1996 Printing

Published by National Textbook Company, a division of NTC Publishing Group.
© 1990 by NTC Publishing Group, 4255 West Touhy Avenue,
Lincolnwood (Chicago), Illinois 60646-1975 U.S.A.

6 7 8 9 ML 9 8 7 6 5 4 3

Contents

Book Three

Preface

Essentials of Reading and Writing English is a three-book series that offers young adult and adult students the opportunity to develop basic reading and writing skills in English. In addition, the material in these books will help students to improve their pronunciation as they become familiar with the sounds of English and the ways in which these sounds correspond to the written language. The three books in this series may be used independently or as a set by students of English as a first or second language who want to acquire basic reading and writing skills in English.

Essentials of Reading and Writing English teaches students to read English using a phonetic approach because English is a phonetic language: all the words in the English language are formed from a combination of the twenty-six letters of the alphabet, and the sounds of these letters are limited and predictable.

Book One presents the alphabet in print, script, and book type, plus one-syllable, three-letter, short-vowel words and sentences. Book Two emphasizes multisyllabic short-vowel words, blends, special sounds, endings, and related sight words. Book Three covers long-vowel words and sentences, special sounds, and related sight words. Each of the three books includes original stories focusing on the special sounds, words, idioms, and grammatical forms taught in that book. Thus, even at the earliest stages of reading development, students experience success and find pleasure in reading the stories in their books.

Essentials of Reading and Writing English, with its clear format and easy-to-follow approach, simplifies the task of learning to read, write, and pronounce English. We have grouped words into meaningful patterns and provided a means of building essential reading and writing skills in English by presenting material in small, easily mastered increments. At the same time, the series offers mastery of a very complex curriculum. At the conclusion of Book Three, students can read, write, and pronounce the major sounds and words in English. They have learned basic vocabulary of home, school, medicine, law, commerce, recreation, and the workplace; and they have learned it in a way that enables them to read and pronounce it most easily.

Through the use of the three books in the *Essentials of Reading and Writing English* series, students will experience increased self-confidence and find success and pleasure in learning to read and write English.

Judith S. Rubenstein and Janet M. Gubbay

Acknowledgments

I want to express my gratitude to those persons and teachers in the field of education who have had the greatest influence on me: Dr. John B. Carroll, Roy Edward Larsen Professor of Educational Psychology, Emeritus, and former Director of the Laboratory for Research in Instruction, Harvard Graduate School of Education, and Dr. Fletcher G. Watson, Henry Lee Shattuck Professor of Education, Emeritus, Harvard Graduate School of Education, both of whom inspired and guided my graduate work; Eloise Gredler who, in her home-school, demonstrated to me the power of phonics for teaching reading; my students, who stimulated me to create materials that could help them, and on whom I tested the lessons in these books; Rebecca Rauff, ESL/EFL Editor, National Textbook Company, who so carefully and skillfully edited the manuscripts; Kathleen Schultz, ESL/EFL Editor, National Textbook Company, who provided valuable assistance in the final stages of the project; and finally, as always, Janet M. Gubbay, my co-author.

These volumes could not have been realized, however, without the support of my family. I am especially grateful to my husband, Howard S. Rubenstein, for his enthusiasm for this project from the start and for many helpful suggestions; to my children, Emily, Adam, Jennifer, and John, for their overall sense of humor and cooperation and spontaneous contributions of ideas; and to both my mother, Martha K. Selig, and my father, the late Dr. Kalman Selig, whose love of books and learning has been my ultimate teacher.

Judith S. Rubenstein

Introduction

The *Essentials of Reading and Writing English* program progresses from the simple to the complex, item by item, chapter by chapter, unit by unit, and book by book. Each chapter and unit builds on the previous ones and is a prerequisite for the next. As students begin in Book One, no assumption is made as to students' abilities, except their ability to see, hear, speak some language, and hold an object in their fingers.

The Phonetic Approach

Essentials of Reading and Writing English teaches students to read English using a phonetic approach because

- English is a phonetic language: all the words of the alphabet are formed from combinations of the twenty-six letters of the alphabet.

- The sounds of the letters are limited and predictable. In addition, the sounds are organized into phonetic rules.

Occasionally there are exceptions to the sounds of the letters, but these exceptions are finite in number, tend to fall into patterns of their own, and can be recognized, learned, and used to predict the sounds of other words.

The words that follow the phonetic rules are called *sound words*. Readers can predict their sounds by applying the rules they have learned for individual letters; they can literally sound out words. Exceptions to the rules are called *sight words*. Readers cannot apply the rules they have learned to predict the sounds of these words; they must be learned by sight.

The phonetic approach provides students with the greatest power to predict the pronunciation of the largest number of new words, giving them an immediate sense of success and the feeling of control over the language.

The power of the phonetic element soon becomes apparent to new readers. After learning only one sound for each of twenty-six letters (twenty-one consonants, five vowels), readers can predict the sound of more than two thousand three-letter, short-vowel words or syllables. For example:

				Words	Syllables
h	a	s		has	mis
b	e	g		hat	seg
p	i	n		beg	sen
c	o	b	=	bet	han
r	u	t		pig	hab
m		l		pin	pol
s		c		cob	rec

$(21 \times 5 \times 21)$

Once they have the power to predict so much, readers are willing to accept the smaller, finite list of unpredictable sight words that must be learned by rote. Teachers can assure beginning students that rules that are easy to understand and use will help them sound out more complicated words. Even the most elementary reading student need be told only that a word is a sound word that can be sounded out or a sight word that must be memorized to feel a sense of control, potential accomplishment, and mastery.

Goals of the Books

Book One is designed for students who need to build fundamental skills. At the completion of Book One, students will have learned to

- read and write the alphabet

- read, pronounce, and write hundreds of one-syllable, three-letter words and sentences, such as *Kim can run*

- predict the sounds of hundreds of additional short-vowel syllables

- read, pronounce, and write twenty-eight basic sight words

- read and understand twenty common idiomatic expressions

- understand and use basic life skills information

By combining the phonetic approach with the memorization of several vital sight words, students will have learned to read and write important examples of the following grammatical forms:

- present tense of the verb *to be*

- subject, object, and possessive pronouns

- types of sentences, including declarative, interrogative, imperative, exclamatory, compound, conditional, future tense, past tense, comparative, idiomatic, and quotation

Students will also have read hundreds of sentences and nine stories composed of vocabulary with the phonetic elements they have learned.

Book Two is designed for students who have completed Book One or for students with some basic skills in English. At the completion of Book Two, students will have learned to

- read, pronounce, and write hundreds of two-syllable, short-vowel words and sentences, such as *Melvin patted his kitten*

- read, pronounce, and write over two hundred words with three or more syllables

- read, pronounce, and write words with special sounds

- read, pronounce, and write words with initial blends, final blends, and with other word endings

- form words with the **ing, ed,** and **er** endings

- read, pronounce, and write sixty-two sight words

- read and understand twenty-seven idiomatic expressions introduced in Book Two, and thirty-five additional idioms using the phonetic elements learned in Book Two

Students will also have learned to read and write important examples of the following grammatical forms:

- functions of the final **s** in third-person singular verbs, possessive nouns, and plural nouns

- thirteen common contractions

Students will also have read hundreds of sentences and twelve stories composed of vocabulary with the phonetic elements they have learned. The style of the stories goes beyond the standard paragraph to include newspaper formats, work lists, and quotations.

Book Three is designed for students who have completed Books One and Two or for students with basic skills in English. At the completion of Book Three, students will have learned to

- read, pronounce, and write hundreds of long-vowel words and sentences, such as *Amy drove to the hotel*

- read, pronounce, and write words with additional letter combinations that make the long-vowel sounds

- read, pronounce, and write words with letter combinations (vowel and consonant) that make special sounds

- read, pronounce, and write important exceptions to sounds and spellings in "Word Alert" sections

Students will also have read sentences and stories incorporating names, geography, idioms, and proverbs while emphasizing a particular sound. The style of the stories goes beyond the standard paragraph to include a newsletter, a checklist, a Help Wanted ad, a cover letter, and a résumé.

Methodology

Every concept in this literacy program, whether sound, word, or sentence, is taught in three stages: *Read, Write,* and *Listen and write.*

- The *Read* section provides practice in sounding out, reading, and comparing the target sounds with other sounds.

- The *Write* section provides reinforcement in reading by encouraging students to observe the word and then reproduce it. The program provides writing practice in the book at the site of the lesson near the book type. It also gives students the opportunity to see the relationship between his or her printing or writing and book type.

- The *Listen and write* section may be used in two ways:

    as intensive practice in ear training, it can be used by students to master the phonetic elements, to learn to spell, and to predict other words;

    as a test, it is a measuring tool with which both students and teachers can evaluate progress and identify areas that require more practice.

Format

All lessons in *Essentials of Reading and Writing English** are presented in an adult format:

- The format is similar to the formats used in newspapers, magazines, mail, and books.

- The lines and spaces provided for students to write are standard size. From the beginning of Book One, students learn to work with lines and spaces that are commonly found on typical forms at a bank, doctor's office, school, employment agency, or government office.

- The reading passages reflect adult responsibilities and real-life situations.

- The illustrations are realistic and recognizable.

Teacher and Student Aids

A handy, two-sided **Alphabet Summary Chart** is included in Book One and may be referred to at any point throughout the program. This two-color chart shows the twenty-six uppercase and lowercase letters in hand printing and script. Through easy-to-follow numbered arrows, stroke order is illustrated and reinforced.

Footnotes are included where necessary to further explain or clarify a particular lesson or an idea in a lesson. These are to assist the teacher on the spot, and provide information that will enhance the teaching of the lesson.

Various **symbols** are included to facilitate the students' learning. It is important that students understand what the following marks symbolize. Throughout the books, the symbols should be pointed out whenever they appear until students are comfortable with them. The teacher may write this chart on the board and have students copy it for reference:

˘ marks the short-vowel sound

‾ marks the long-vowel sound

= means that one sound equals (sounds the same as) another sound

The following **classroom tools** will be helpful in the literacy classroom:

- a world map

- a map of the United States with state boundaries marked

These reference materials bring to life the geographical information taught in this program. Teachers and students will enjoy checking the maps as places are referred to in the books.

Learners Who Can Benefit from This Literacy Program

Essentials of Reading and Writing English is a versatile literacy program that can be used by students with a variety of needs and backgrounds:

1. *Native English speakers* who understand the meaning of the words in this program, but cannot read or write them, can use the books as reading and writing textbook-workbooks, starting at the beginning of Book One and pro-

---

*Teachers may want to explain to students that the ampersand (&) used in the title on the cover and title page stands for *and*. It is sometimes used in titles and signs, but is not used in prose.

gressing through each lesson in the program. Students can teach themselves to read the letters of the alphabet in six forms, to form the letters in both print and script, and to write the exercises in whichever form they think is most appropriate. The program is adaptable to a variety of learning situations. Students may progress through the program independently, with a tutor or literacy volunteer, or in a classroom environment.

2. *Elementary students of English as a Second Language* who do not speak, read, or write English well, do not understand the meaning of the words in this program, and want to learn standard conversation patterns not included in these books can use the books as textbook-workbooks complementary to conversation lessons. While part of class time can be spent in conversation, the part allocated to reading and writing can begin with Book One, starting at the beginning of the book and working through to the end. As phonetic rules are learned, the teacher can point out how certain elements of the conversation units are examples of recently learned phonetic rules.

3. *Intermediate and advanced students of English as a Second Language* who read and write well and have a large written vocabulary, but poor pronunciation and little fluency in speaking can use the books for speaking practice. In Book One, each chapter concentrates on a vowel sound, enabling students to practice and correct their pronunciation. For example, for speakers who say, "Jeem beet thee peet," instead of "Jim bit the pit," Chapter 3 provides over a hundred sounds, words, statements, and questions, and a story emphasizing the correct sound of the short-vowel sound $\breve{\imath}$. Other vowel and consonant sounds and combinations are emphasized in Books Two and Three; for example **ed** = $\breve{\imath}d$, **t**, **d** in *patted, jumped, clanged.*

For all students, *Essentials of Reading and Writing English* genuinely simplifies the task of learning to read, write, and pronounce English by being easy to understand, grouping words into meaningful patterns, and building by small, masterable increments. Nonetheless, it has for its end result the mastery of a very complex curriculum.

Overall, through phonics, students have learned that English is an organized and rational language with rules from which they can make multiple predictions. Most importantly, through the *Essentials of Reading and Writing English* basic English literacy program, students will develop a positive, optimistic attitude toward reading and writing English.

Use of This Manual

This teacher's manual contains a separate section for each of the three books in the *Essentials of Reading and Writing English* literacy program. The section for each book is divided into two main parts: important introductory material followed by specific guidelines for each chapter in the book.

The introductory material discusses the contents and the objectives of each part of the book; how to use the major teaching devices that are used repeatedly in that book, with examples from specific pages; and how to use the major text sections or chapters.

The guidelines that follow emphasize the major concept and objective of each page or group of pages, and provide specific suggestions for teaching the material. These guidelines include variations of and exceptions to presentation, instructional sequence, or teaching strategy; items to compare and contrast; and supplementary material.

The teacher can derive maximum benefit from this manual by reading the introductory section of each book first and then referring back to it when indicated in the page-by-page guidelines for the book.

Book One
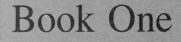

Book One contains Units I–III with fourteen chapters, Appendices A–C, and nine stories.

Objectives of Book One

Unit One: **The Alphabet**	Develops preliteracy skills by presenting the component shapes of letters Presents the alphabet: sounds; uppercase and lowercase letters in book type, hand printing, and script
Chapter 1: **Shapes of Letters**	Develops eye/hand coordination, left-to-right Presents the component shapes of letters
Chapter 2: **The Alphabet**	Presents: • the twenty-six letters of the English alphabet: all the basic sounds of each letter with emphasis on the short-vowel or hard consonant sound • the six written forms of each letter: uppercase and lowercase for book type, hand printing, and script
Unit Two: **Short-Vowel Words**	Presents one-syllable words for each of the five short vowels and related sight words in word lists, sentences, and stories for students to *Read*, *Write*, and *Listen and write*
Chapter 3: **Words with the ĭ Sound**	Presents words, sentences, and a story with the short sound of the vowel **i** and related sight words
Chapter 4: **Words with the ă Sound**	Presents words, sentences, and a story with the short sound of the vowel **a** and related sight words
Chapter 5: **Review of the ă and ĭ Sounds**	Reviews, contrasts, and clarifies the differences between the short-vowel sounds ă and ĭ
Chapter 6: **Words with the ŏ Sound**	Presents words, sentences, and a story with the short sound of the vowel **o** and related sight words
Chapter 7: **Review of the ă, ĭ, and ŏ Sounds**	Reviews, contrasts, and clarifies the differences between the short-vowel sounds ă, ĭ, and ŏ
Chapter 8: **Words with the ŭ Sound**	Presents words, sentences, and a story with the short sound of the vowel **u** and related sight words
Chapter 9: **Review of the ă, ĭ, ŏ, and ŭ Sounds**	Reviews, contrasts, and clarifies the differences between the short-vowel sounds ă, ĭ, ŏ and ŭ
Chapter 10: **Words with the ĕ Sound**	Presents words, sentences, and a story with the short sound of the vowel **e** and related sight words
Chapter 11: **Review of the ă, ĕ, ĭ, ŏ, and ŭ Sounds**	Reviews, contrasts, and clarifies the differences between the short-vowel sounds ă, ĕ, ĭ, ŏ, and ŭ

Unit Three: **Life Skills**	Presents information necessary to daily life: numbers, colors, personal identification
Chapter 12: **Numbers**	Presents: • a counting summary chart of numbers 1 through 100 • equivalent dots for 0 through 9 • forms of representative numbers from zero through one billion (digits and words in book type, hand printing, and script) • the calendar: days, months, and abbreviations • the clock: face and digital; A.M., P.M., hour; quarter, half, and three-quarter hours; odd minutes before and after the hour; midnight, noon, and alternative ways of saying the time
Chapter 13: **Colors**	Presents the names of twelve basic colors in book type, hand printing, and script
Chapter 14: **Personal Identification**	Presents: • common abbreviations (titles, places, others) • information regarding name, country, nationality, address, telephone number, social security number, and job in three handwritten forms: uppercase and lowercase printing, all uppercase printing, and script
Appendices	Provide a summary and review of the information presented in Book One for students and teacher to use as reference material and as a source for generating new sentences and additional exercises
Appendix A: **Scope and Sequence Charts**	Provides a separate scope and sequence chart for each of the five short-vowel sounds *(ă, ĕ, ĭ, ŏ, ŭ)*, listing all the words in the text (and some additional ones) with that sound by categories: proper nouns, verbs, adjectives, nouns, pronouns, prepositions, other (conjunctions, interjections, adverbs, prefixes, articles, titles)
Appendix B: **Sight Words Grouped by Vowel Sounds**	Presents sight words in meaningful groups, using: short-vowel sounds students have learned *(ă, ĕ, ĭ, ŏ, ŭ)*; long-vowel sounds that have been introduced *(ā, ē, ī, ō, ū)*; other vowel sounds that will be taught in Books Two and Three *(o͝o, o͞o, ä, er)*
Appendix C: **Idioms**	Presents twenty common idioms that use the five short vowels and sight words taught in Book One, with definitions and sample sentences

Stories	Book One contains nine stories, one for each chapter in Unit Two. The stories use the specific phonetic elements and sight words taught in the chapter, and include for review phonetic elements and sight words from earlier chapters.
	    The themes of these stories center on adult concerns such as work and relationships with family, friends, and colleagues within the limits of the vocabulary and the phonetic elements students have learned.
	    If students have mastered the pages preceding the stories, they will be able to read them with ease. In fact, they will be amazed at the high level of

complexity and achievement they have reached, even early in the book. The stories throughout the program provide a great reward for learning.

How to Use the Major Teaching Devices

Three major teaching devices (the *Read, Write,* and *Listen and write* sections) appear throughout the book and are the foundation of the *Essentials of Reading and Writing English* program.

Read

How to Use the *Read* Section

The mechanism of the *Read* section is basically the same for *Sounds, Words, Sentences,* and *Stories.*

In all cases, concentrate on the sound of the letter. When reading an individual sound, say the sound the letter makes, not the name of the letter. For example, on page 8 of the student text, say *ă* (as in *apple*), not the letter name **A.** On page 36, read *bi, di (bih, dih),* not *bee-eye, dee-eye.* Always start by reading the target sound, then build the words on the sound.

The following are some successful reading strategies:

1. *Teacher reads first.* Read some examples to students. Have them listen and repeat what you read. Say:

Listen to the (sounds/words/sentences) I will read. Listen especially for the (new/vowel) sounds. Look at the (sounds/words/sentences) while I read them. Then read them after me.

The advantage of this listen and repeat method, at the beginning, is that students can match sounds with letters. The disadvantage is that students may tend to chant and chorus by rote what they have just heard, rather than read it. So it is important to advance to student-initiated reading, the next step.

2. *Students read first.* The teacher then repeats and corrects the pronunciation. The student reading may be individual (preferable) or group (if necessary). Use either or both of the following strategies:

   a. Have students read around the room, chain reading. Indicate the order you want to use, having each student read one sound, word, or sentence in turn.

   b. If students' attention wanders, do not preassign order. Call on them in random order. Not knowing when they will be called on will encourage them to follow along as the reading progresses.

> **Note**
> Throughout the lesson, make sure that students' pronunciation is correct (or at least being attempted). Also check to ensure that students understand that particular letters represent particular sounds.

Write

How to Use the *Write* Section

The mechanism of the *Write* section is basically the same for *Sounds, Words, Sentences,* and *Stories.*

1. Have students write only after reading. Decide if they should write after each item or at the end of the *Read* section. (Usually, it is preferable to write immediately after each item.)

2. Allow students to use either hand printing or script.

Note

Encourage the use of script, since it is the most accepted form of handwritten communication, especially for adults. However, do not discourage printing if it will enable the reading to progress more smoothly. You and the students can always return to any point in the text to practice writing a passage in script. The object of the *Write* section is dual—to reinforce the reading and to write.

---

3. In the *Write* section, have students *copy* the words, not write them from memory. Encourage them to look back at the printed letters in the text before they write. This technique helps reinforce the similarities and differences between book type, hand printing, and script. Students will write from memory in the *Listen and write* section.

4. Encourage students to say each sound quietly to themselves as they write it.

5. Walk among the group to provide assistance, immediate correction, reassurance, and support.

Listen and write

How to Use the *Listen and write* Section

The mechanism of the *Listen and write* section is basically the same for *Sounds, Words, Sentences,* and *Stories.*

Listen and write is a critical part of the lesson. It forces students to focus their attention and indicates to them and to you whether or not they know the sound, word, or sentence. Students may think they hear the difference between the sounds, but it is only in *Listen and write* that they will see what they do and do not understand.

Although this section can be used as a test, its main objective is to clarify students' concepts of the sounds before they progress to the next step—a slightly more advanced level.

Listen and write can be rewarding for many students, but very difficult for others. It is not necessary to complete all the *Listen and write* lines. Sometimes doing just a few will make the point. Sometimes all are needed as a review before advancing. Use your discretion in using this teaching tool to facilitate and evaluate your students' progress.

As you begin *Listen and write:*

1. Tell students to use a piece of paper to cover the part of the page that you will be dictating.

2. Dictate any or all of the sounds, words, sentences, or parts of sentences in the *Read* line, either in the order given (fixed order) or in random order (mixed order).

3. Mark the order of the items you use in your own book.

In the Review chapters the *Listen and write* has two parts: fixed order and mixed order. (See "How to Use the Sounds Section" on page 35 of this manual.)

When students have finished, write the list on the board or have volunteers do so. Correct and compliment their attempts. Indicate that you know how difficult this work is, but explain that it will improve students' vocabulary, spelling, and listening skills. Then repeat the exercise, if desired, with a few more items. Any unused space on the paper can be used by students to practice writing the words they missed.

You might find it helpful at first to dictate only two or three items, stop and correct them, then proceed with another two or three. Don't overwhelm students. Never introduce a feeling of failure.

Unit One: The Alphabet

Chapter 1: Shapes of Letters

Pages 2–3
Objectives

- To prepare for learning the English alphabet by discriminating between and learning the component shapes of the letters

- To develop eye/hand coordination, left-to-right

Instructional Sequence

Draw an example on the board without the connecting line. Explain:

English is read from left to right. This is left (point). This is right (point).

Draw a connecting line on the board from left to right. Provide a few more examples.

Ask: Which is your left hand? Which is your right hand?

Demonstrate how your left and right "move" when you face the students and when you turn away. Students may also stand and show left and right (front and back). Explain that the left side of a paper or the board corresponds to their left as they face it.

Direct students' attention to the example at the top of page 2 and point out the two matching shapes (the circles), the one nonmatching shape (the half circle), and the line from left to right connecting the matching shapes. Ask students to match each shape on the left with the one on the right that is the same and to draw a line from the shape on the left to the one on the right. Correct them if they draw from right to left. As students work, walk around the room to provide encouragement.

Do the example at the top of page 3, then have students complete the page, matching three pairs of shapes in each of the four boxes.

Skill Reinforcement and Additional Practice

1. Draw shapes on the board and have volunteers match them from left to right.

2. Ask volunteers to draw shapes on the board some of which match. Ask other volunteers to match the shapes by drawing connecting lines from left to right.

Pages 4–5
Objectives

- To recognize basic shapes

- To discriminate one shape from different but related shapes

- To circle basic shapes

- To write basic shapes

Instructional Sequence

Draw circles (on the board and in the air), starting at the two o'clock position and moving counterclockwise, up and back. Emphasize that this stroke is essential for forming letters. Discourage students from circling clockwise.

Direct attention to the first line of the lesson. Point to the example and ask students to circle the shapes that are the same as the example, moving from left to right. You may want to do the first line with them. Then have them write that shape on the next line. You may want to do a few examples on the board.

Skill Reinforcement and Additional Practice

1. Ask a few volunteers to draw lines of shapes on the board some of which match. Ask other volunteers to circle the matching shapes on each line.

2. Have volunteers draw the shapes that are different from the first ones on the lines of the lesson, either on the board or on paper.

Chapter 2: The Alphabet

Page 6   ## Objective

To summarize and differentiate between the twenty-six uppercase and lowercase letters of the English alphabet in hand printing and book type

Instructional Sequence

Say:

This chart shows the twenty-six letters of the English alphabet as you would print them. Each letter has two printed forms: uppercase (capital) and lowercase (small). Notice the difference between book type and hand printing.

Reassure students that they will be learning only one letter at a time. Emphasize that this reference chart allows them to see all the printed letters together. Do not attempt to have students master this chart now. Come back to it after completing the *Alphabet* section or to compare and contrast letters as they are introduced.

Page 7   ## Objective

To summarize and differentiate between the twenty-six uppercase and lowercase letters of the English alphabet in script and in book type.

> **Note**
> The hand printing and script alphabets have been systematically revised to make learning easier. Each student usually develops a characteristic style. Therefore, unnecessary decorative (and potentially confusing) flourishes have been removed, making the script alphabet as similar to the printed one as possible, yet retaining enough script character to resemble other common styles of script.

Instructional Sequence

Say:

This chart shows the twenty-six letters of the English alphabet as you would write them in script. Each letter has two written forms: uppercase (capital) and lowercase (small). Notice the difference between book type and script (handwritten form).

Reassure students that they will be learning only one letter at a time. Do not attempt to have them master this chart now. Come back to it after completing the *Alphabet* section or to compare and contrast letters as they are introduced. Use it for reference.

Pages 8–33 ## Objectives

• To present the twenty-six letters of the English alphabet, one at a time

• To provide all the basic information about each letter on one page

• To read, print, and write six forms of each letter: two book type, two hand printing, two script (uppercase and lowercase of each)

• To print and write each letter in the context of a word

Instructional Sequence

Each *Alphabet* page is designed to integrate reading and writing skills. Have students complete the lesson as a group and/or individually. (As they work individually, walk around the room to provide assistance and encouragement.)

Each *Alphabet* lesson follows the same format. Teaching them in the same way may lessen students' anxiety, since they will be able to predict what to expect. This will allow them to concentrate on content rather than on interpreting directions. The following offers one method for teaching each letter, including successful teacher dialogue and actions:

Say:

This is the letter **A.** It has six forms.

Point to each form at the top of the page and note the differences between uppercase and lowercase letters: two book type forms; two hand printed forms; two script (written) forms.

Say:

The letter **A** makes two main sounds: (point to the example at the top of the page) the short sound *ă* as in *apple* and the long sound *ā* as in *ape.* (Point to the boxes in the middle of the page.) The long sound of the vowel sounds like the name of the letter: *a (ay), e (ee), i (eye), o (oh), u (you).*

Say:

This book focuses on the short sounds. You will learn the other sounds for each letter in Books Two and Three and as sight words in Book One. In this book you will be using only the short sound *ă* as in *apple* (point again to the illustration) unless exceptions are noted, such as sight words (see Appendix B). Unless you are told otherwise, whenever you see the letter **a** in this book say *ă* as in *apple*.

Direct students' attention to the first line of the lesson. Point to book type **a.** Read the short sound *ă* to the class a few times, then read the first line of **a** together with students. Say *ă, ă, ă, ă, ă,* etc. Read the **a** as if it were a word.

Reading Strategy Suggestions

1. Whole class alternates reading with teacher

2. Individuals alternate reading with teacher

3. Individuals read alone

Writing Strategy Suggestions

The following provides sample teacher dialogue and actions:

Hand Printing
Say:

Print small **a** (say *ah,* not *ay*). Emphasize the short sound *ă* to ensure proper usage.

Point to the top line, the bottom line, and the middle line in the printing space in the book. Draw a few examples of **a** on the board.
Say:

Follow the arrows and the numbers. Start the circle just below the middle line.

Point to the two o'clock position and motion upward.
Say:

Trace the dotted small **a**'s. Then fill the line with **a**'s.

Keep repeating the short sound *ă.*
Say:

Read capital **A** (say *ah,* not *ay*). Print capital **A.** Start at the top line. Push down and left. Lift your pencil, go back to the top, push down and right. Then lift up and draw a line from left to right through the center of **A,** just below the middle line. Draw a few examples on the board.

Say:

Trace the capital **A**'s. Fill the line with **A**'s. Keep repeating the short sound *ă*. Circle all the small **a**'s in this line, moving left to right. Point to the two o'clock position and motion upward when drawing a circle.

Say:

Notice the letters that are different but similar. You will learn these letters later.

Say:

Circle all the capital **A**'s in this line, moving left to right. Print a line of small **a**'s like this one. Point to the example. Demonstrate on the board.

Say:

Print a line of capital **A**'s like this one. Point to the example. Demonstrate on the board.

Say:

Complete the word in each box. Trace the dotted small **a.** Remind students that *rain* and *ape* have the long sound *ā.*

Script

Teach script letters when you think students are ready. If they are having trouble with printing, you can complete Book One with printing, then go back to the *Alphabet* pages for script. However, it is desirable to begin script as early as possible, since that is the preferred adult form.

Script letters are closely related to print letters. Point out that the letters are basically the same, with connecting lines. Demonstrate how to follow the arrows and backtrack. Emphasize ease and similarity rather than difficulty and difference.

You may want to ask students to read one line of the *ă* sound first. Note the similarities and differences between the printed **a** and the script **a.**

Before students begin tracing and writing the lowercase script **a,** demonstrate the strokes on the board. Point out that the letter **a** can be at the beginning, middle, or end of a word.

Say:

Start at the bottom and lead into the **a** with this connecting line from the bottom to the top of the letter. Next, push back to the left and down and up to make an open circle for the **a** almost as you did when you printed, except this letter is slanted. Continue pushing your pencil up to the top of the letter and come down again. This downward line is like the straight line in the printed small **a,** but it is slanted. Continue the line in a little hook to the right, which will lead into a connecting line to another letter.

Explain that the basic idea in printing is to lift the pencil between strokes. In script, the pencil is generally not lifted within a word since most of the strokes are connected.
Say:

Trace the two small dotted **a**'s on the line. Then fill the line with small **a**'s.

Say:

Complete each word by tracing the small dotted **a**'s in each word. After students have traced the **a**'s, read the words with them. Point out that the words in the picture boxes match the words they have just completed. Have them compare the print and script forms of each word.

When students are ready, they can practice writing the capital **A** in script. Repeat the steps you used for having them trace, fill the line, and complete the words with the lowercase script **a**.

Skill Reinforcement and Additional Practice

1. Have students find and circle the lowercase **a** in *Adam*.

2. Ask volunteers to print and write capital **A** and small **a** on the board.

3. Cut up and distribute small, manageable sections of a newspaper page. Ask students to locate and circle all of the capital and small **a**'s.

4. If some students have short-vowel **a**'s in their names, you may want to print the names on the board and have the class pronounce them.

Note
Use the same strategies for teaching the rest of the *Alphabet* pages. Variations for special cases and more specific suggestions for teaching each letter are presented below.

Page 8   **The letter A**
See Teacher's Manual pages 12–16. This page is used as the example there.

Page 9   ## The letter B
Say:

The letter **B** makes the sound *b (buh)* as in *bus*. Have students practice this sound as a group and individually.

In the word/picture box and on the script line, have students find and complete the two **b**'s in *baby*.

Page 10   ## The letter C
Say:

The letter **C** makes two main sounds: the hard sound *k* as in *can* (point to *can* in the illustration), and the soft sound *s* as in *cereal* and *city*. In this book, you will be using only the hard sound *k* as in *can* (point again to *can* in the illustration). As a rule, unless you are told otherwise, whenever you see the letter **c** in this book, say *cuh*. You may want to tell students that they will use the *s* sound of soft **c** *(cereal, city)* in Book Two. Emphasize *c (cuh)* throughout the lesson. Have students practice as a group and individually.

In the word/picture boxes, and on the script line, have students find and complete the two **c**'s in *clock* and in *circle*. Point out that the two **c**'s in *clock* are examples of the hard *k* sound of **c**, but that the first **c** in *circle* has the soft *s* sound and the second **c** has the hard *k* sound. Print *circle* on the board and point to each **c** as you talk about it.

When students have completed the last line of the page, call attention to the name *Chen*. Explain that **c** + **h** makes the special sound *ch*, which they will learn and use in Book Two.

Skill Reinforcement and Additional Practice

1. Print or write *clock* and *circle* on the board. Ask volunteers to point to the **c** sound you say.

2. With *clock* and *circle* on the board, ask for two volunteers to circle the sound of **c** they hear the class say. Prompt the class to pronounce first one sound, then the other. (Emphasize the hard *k* sound of **c**.)

Page 11   ## The letter D
Say:

The letter **D** makes the sound *d (duh)* as in *dollar*.

Before students read the line of small **d**'s, point out that the letter **d** is the opposite of the letter **b**. Have them turn to page 9 to contrast **d** with **b**. Before they read the line of capital **D**'s, point out that capital **D** has one loop, but that capital **B** has two loops. Print both letters on the board, or have students turn to page 6 to compare and contrast **B** and **D**.

Before students find and circle the lowercase **d**'s, remind them to look out for lowercase **b**'s.

When students are ready to read and complete the word/picture boxes, call attention to the word *bed* and point out that *bed* has both a **b** and a **d**.

Page 12   ## The letter E
Say:

The letter **E** makes two main sounds: the short sound ĕ as in *egg* (point to the illustration), and the long sound ē as in *teeth* (point to the illustration). The long sound ē sounds like the name of the letter **E.** In this book, you will be using only the short sound ĕ as in *egg* (point again to the illustration). As a rule, unless you are told otherwise, whenever you see the letter **e** in this book, say ĕ as in *egg*. Exceptions are noted, such as *the* (**e** = ŭ) and *live* (**e** is silent).

When students are ready to read and complete the script line, point out the two **e**'s in *Ellen*, noting that one is a capital and the other is small, but that both have the ĕ as in *egg* sound.

Page 13   ## The letter F
Say:

The letter **F** makes the sound *f (fuh)* as in *fish*.

Point to the illustrations at the top of the page and in the word/picture box.

You may want to have students compare and contrast the capital letters **F** and **E**. Point out their differences and similarities (**F** has only two horizontal lines). When they are ready to read and complete the word/picture boxes, point out that *cuff* has two **f**'s. Explain that two **f**'s together have one sound—*fuh* as in *fish*.

Page 14   ## The letter G
Say:

The letter **G** makes two sounds: the hard sound *guh* as in *gas* (point to the illustration at the top of the page), *got,* and *gum,* and the soft sound *juh* as in *gem* and *ginger*. In this book, you will be using only the hard sound *guh* as in *gas* (point again to the illustration of the gas pump).

Print a lowercase **g** on the board and say:

Begin this letter with a small **c** and add a tail.

Print a capital **G** on the board and say:

Begin this letter like a capital **C** and add a line going in to the middle.

You might want to have students turn to page 10 and compare and contrast the capital and small forms of **C** and **G**.

When they are ready to complete the last line on the page, point out that the names *George* and *Gina* have the soft *juh* sound of **g** as in *gem* and *ginger*. Explain that they will learn and use this sound in Book Two. Emphasize throughout the lesson that the letter **G** makes the hard sound *guh* as in *gas* when used in Book One, unless exceptions are noted.

Page 15   The letter H
Say:

The letter **H** makes the sound ***huh*** as in *hat* (point to the illustration).

You may want to have students compare and contrast capital **A** and **H**. Point out that the sides of **H** are straight, while the sides of **A** are slanted. As an example, print *HAT* on the board in capital letters.

Page 16   The letter I
Say:

The letter **I** makes two main sounds: the short sound $\breve{i}$ as in *inch* (point to the illustration at the top of the page), and the long sound $\bar{i}$ as in *ice* and *iron* (point to the illustration of *iron* in the word/picture box). The long sound $\bar{i}$ sounds like the name of the letter **I**. In this book, you will be using only the short sound $\breve{i}$ as in *inch*, unless exceptions are noted, such as sight words *said* and *I*. As a rule, unless you are told otherwise, whenever you see the letter **i** in this book, say $\breve{i}$ as in *inch*. You will learn and use the long sound $\bar{i}$ as in *ice* and *iron* in Book Three. (Students will learn **i** $= \bar{e}$ as in *Maria* in Book Three.)

Have students compare and contrast capital **I** with **E** and **F**.
Emphasize the short sound $\breve{i}$ as in *inch* throughout the lesson.

Page 17   The letter J
Say:

The letter **J** makes the sound ***juh*** as in *jet*. Point to the illustrations at the top of the page and in the word/picture box.

Have students compare and contrast **J** with **I**.

Page 18   The letter K
Say:

The letter **K** makes the sound ***kuh*** as in *kitchen*. Point to the illustrations at the top of the page and in the word/picture box.

Have students compare **K** especially with **A**, **E**, **F**, and **H**.

Page 19   ## The letter L
Say:

The letter **L** makes the sound *luh* as in *leg*. Point to the illustrations at the top of the page and in the word/picture box.

When students are ready to read and complete the word/picture boxes, point out that *shell* has two **l**'s, and tell them that two **l**'s together have one sound—*luh* as in *leg*.

Have students compare and contrast **L** especially with **I, J, E,** and **F.**

Page 20   ## The letter M
Say:

The letter **M** makes the sound *muh* as in *man*. Point to the illustrations at the top of the page and in the word/picture box. You may want to have a few of the men in your class stand one at a time as you say *man*.

> **Note**
> *Printed* **M:** Note the order of the strokes in the hand-printed form of capital **M.** This variation of the traditional way of teaching this letter is the easiest for students to learn and the most similar to script.

Page 21   ## The letter N
Say:

The letter **N** makes the sound *nuh* as in *nut*. Point to the illustrations at the top of the page and in the word/picture box.

> **Note**
> *Printed* **N:** Note the order of the strokes in the hand-printed form of capital **N.** This variation of the traditional way of teaching this letter is the easiest for students to learn and the most similar to script.

Have students compare and contrast the capital and lowercase letters **M/m** and **N/n.** Point out that **N/n** has one fewer loop (and is smaller) than **M/m** in both the hand-printed and script forms.

Page 22   ## The letter O
Say:

The letter **O** has two main sounds: the short sound ŏ as in *octopus* (point to the illustrations at the top of the page and in the sound/letter box) and the long sound ō as in *ocean* and *boat* (point to the illustration of *boat* in the word/picture box). The long ō sounds like the name of the letter **o.** In this book you will be using only the short sound ŏ as in *octopus,* unless exceptions are noted, such as sight words *to, do.* As a rule, unless you are told otherwise, whenever you see the letter **o** in this book, you will say ŏ as in *octopus.* You will learn and use the long sound ō as in *ocean* in Book Two and the long sound of *boat* in Book Three.

Note
Explain that the sound of the **c** in *ocean* is an exception and sounds like *sh.* (See Book Three, page 202.)

Emphasize the short sound ŏ as in *octopus* throughout the lesson.
Have students compare and contrast **O/o** especially with **C, D, G** and **c, d, g, b.**

Page 23   The letter P
Say:

The letter **P** makes the sound **puh** as in *pig.* Point to the illustrations at the top of the page and in the word/picture box. Point out that *pup* in the word/picture box has two **p**'s.

Have students compare and contrast **P/p** especially with **B/b** and **D/d.**

Page 24   The letter Q
Say:

The letter **Q** is always followed by **u** in English. **Qu** together say *kwuh.* Point to the **qu** in words on the page and say **kwuh** as in *quilt.*

Have students compare and contrast **Q/q** especially with **O, C, G, D** and **p, b, d.**

Page 25   The letter R
Say:

The letter **R** makes the sound **ruh** as in *rug.* Point to the illustrations at the top of the page and in the word/picture box.

Have students compare and contrast **R/r** especially with **P, B, D** and **p, b, d.**

Page 26   The letter S
Say:

The letter **S** makes the sound **suh** as in *sun.* Point to the illustrations at the top of the page and in the word/picture box.

Have students compare and contrast **S/s** especially with **C/c.**

Page 27   ## The letter T
Say:

The letter **T** makes the sound *tuh* as in *television.* Point to the illustrations at the top of the page and in the word/picture box. Tell students that the word *television* is often abbreviated to *TV,* the actual sound of both letter names.

Have students compare and contrast **T/t** in script with **T** and **F,** and hand-printed **T/t** especially with **H, I, J, L** and **l, i, j.**

Page 28   ## The letter U
Say:

The letter **U** makes two main sounds: the short sound **ŭ** as in *umbrella* (point to the illustrations at the top of the page and in the word/ picture box), and the long sound **ū** as in *tube* (point to the illustration in the word/picture box). The long **ū** sounds like the name of the letter **u.** In this book you will be using only the short sound **ŭ** as in *umbrella,* unless exceptions are noted such as sight word *full.* As a rule, unless you are told otherwise, whenever you see the letter **u** in this book, say **ŭ** as in *umbrella.* You will learn and use the long sound **ū** as in *tube* in Book Three.

Have students compare and contrast **U/u** especially with **C/c, O/o.**

Page 29   ## The letter V
Say:

The letter **V** makes the sound *vuh* as in *van.* Point to the illustrations at the top of the page and in the word/picture box.

> **Note**
> *Hand-printed* **V:** Note the order of the strokes in the hand-printed form of **v.** This varies from the traditional way of teaching this letter; however, the continuous down-up movement (without lifting the pencil) is the easiest for students to learn and the most similar to script.

Have students compare and contrast **V/v** especially with **U/u.**

Page 30   ## The letter W
Say:

The letter **W** makes the sound *wuh* as in *wig.* Point to the illustrations at the top of the page and in the word/picture box.

> **Note**
> *Hand-printed* **W:** Note the order of the strokes in the hand-printed form of **W/w.** This varies from the traditional way of teaching this letter; however, the continuous down-up movement (without lifting the pencil) is the easiest for students to learn and the most similar to script.

Have students compare and contrast **W/w** and **V/v.** Point out that **W/w** has one more "V" (and is bigger) than **V/v** in both the hand-printed forms.

Page 31   ## The letter X
Say:

The letter **X** makes two main sounds: the sound *ks* as in *box* (point to the illustrations at the top of the page and in the word/picture box), and the sound *z* as in *xylophone* (point to the illustration in the word/picture box.). In this book you will be using only the *ks* sound of **x** as in *box*. You will learn and use the *z* sound of **x** as in *xylophone* in Book Three.

Have students compare **X/x** especially with **N/n, M/m, W/w, V/v.**

Page 32   ## The letter Y
Say:

The letter **Y** makes four sounds: the sound *yuh* as in *yam* (point to the illustrations at the top of the page and in the word/picture box); the sound *ē* as in *baby* and *cherry* (point to the illustrations in the word/picture box); the sound *ī* as in *sky* (like the *ī* in *ice* and *iron*); the sound *ĭ* as in *syrup* (like the *ĭ* in *inch*). In this book, you will be using only the *yuh* sound of *yam*, except for the sight word *they*. You will learn and use the other sounds of **y** in Books Two and Three.

Have students compare and contrast **Y/y** especially with **V/v, X/x, W/w, U/u, N/n.**

Page 33   ## The letter Z
Say:

The letter **Z** makes the sound *zuh* as in *zipper*.

Point to the illustrations at the top of the page and in the word/picture box. Have students compare and contrast **Z/z** especially with **X/x, Y/y, N/n, V/v, W/w.**

Page 34   ## Double Consonants

Objectives

• To understand that two identical (double) consonants at the end of a word make one sound

• To read and write twelve one-syllable words with double consonants

Unit Two: Short-Vowel Words

Unit Two* consists of nine chapters (3–11)—one chapter for each of the five short vowels and four review chapters. The vowel chapters follow one pattern; the review chapters follow another pattern. This uniformity of chapter design facilitates teaching and learning.

In this unit, short-vowel words are taught in the order of complexity of the vowels beginning with **i**, (*ĭ*), the basis of common, small, phonetic words, for example, *it, is, in,* and ending with **e**, (*ĕ*), the short-vowel sound that most frequently presents difficulty in reading.

Most of the vocabulary words in this unit are used in everyday speech, for example, *can, will, not, red, cup.* Several words are less common, for example, *keg, nip, tug,* but help teach a phonetic principle, and provide students with invaluable practice. Many of the sound words make up common idioms, for example, *up to it.* These idiomatic expressions are incorporated throughout the book and are listed in Appendix C.

This section of the manual contains general discussions of how to use the vowel chapters and the review chapters, followed by specific teaching suggestions for each chapter in Unit Two. Read the general discussions first, then refer to the specific suggestions for each chapter as you teach it.

How to Use the Vowel Chapters

Objectives

To read and write words, sentences, and a story with the short-vowel sound and related sight words

Each vowel chapter is composed of the following skill-building sections:

- **Sounds** (introduces the vowel sound and presents an illustrated example word)

- **Sounds and Words** (contains a summary chart of words with the vowel sound and every initial consonant with which it commonly occurs. Also includes a list of related *Sight Words.*)

- **Words** (provides practice in reading, writing, and writing from memory short-vowel words)

- **Read, Circle, Write** (provides an opportunity to read, write, and demonstrate comprehension of short-vowel phrases)

- **Sight Words** (when appropriate)

- **Special Sounds** (when appropriate)

- **Special Skills** (when appropriate)

---

*Integrate lessons from Unit Three: Life Skills at any point after the *Alphabet* pages. For example, you may want to teach some numbers after Chapter 3 (*ĭ*) and after Chapter 5 (review of *ă* and *ĭ*). See page 49 of this manual.

- **Sentences: Statements** (contains twenty-four statement sentences that emphasize the short-vowel words)

- **Sentences: Questions** (contains twenty-four question sentences that emphasize the short-vowel words)

- **Story** (presents the short-vowel words in a thematic context)

- **Bonus Page** (contains additional exercises that may be used as a test, as extra practice, or as supplementary material for students who are progressing more quickly than the rest of the class)

A discussion of how to use each of these sections follows. *Chapter 3: Words with the ĭ Sound* is used as the example in this discussion.

Sounds

How to Use the *Sounds* Section
(for example, see page 36)

Introduce the sound.
 Say:

This is *ĭ* as in *inch*. Point to the picture at the top right corner of the page.

If you have a ruler, point to an inch on it and pass it around the room.

It is important that you emphasize and students read the sound of the letter (*ĭ* as in *inch*) and not the name of the letter (*ī [eye]* as in *ice*). This also pertains to all vowels taught in later chapters.

Read: Read the first line to the class, emphasizing the short-vowel *ĭ* sound. Explain that these are lines of the *ĭ* sound combined with common consonants, for example *bĭ (bih), dĭ (dih), fĭ (fih),* . . . When you have read as much as necessary, alternate reading with the class. (Refer to "How to Use the *Read* Section" on page 10 of this manual.) If appropriate for your class, have individuals say two or more sounds aloud.

Write: Have students copy the two lines of *ĭ* sounds. (See "How to Use the *Write* Section" on pages 10–11 of this manual for suggestions.)

Listen and write: See "How to Use the *Listen and write* Section" on pages 11–12 of this manual for suggestions.

Sounds and Words

How to Use the *Sounds and Words* Section
(for example, see page 36)

This short-vowel chart provides:

- the target sound preceded by every relevant consonant

- the target sound embedded in a short-vowel word

> **Note**
> Some consonant-vowel combinations are excluded because they are not common sounds in English. Others will be taught in Books Two and Three. (For example, *ci* as in *city* and *ce* as in *cent* with the soft sound of **c** are taught in Book Two.)

Instructional Sequence

1. Students listen to the ĭ sound in each word as you read it.

2. Students read each line of sounds and words with you.

3. Class reads each line as you listen (after giving them an initial prompt).

4. Individuals read one line apiece.
   The following provides sample teacher dialogue and actions.
Say:

Listen to the ĭ sound in each word. Call attention to the fact that the **i** is boldfaced (in darker print than the other letters in the word). Point to the chart and read: **b (buh), bĭ (bih),** *bid, big, bill, Bill, bin, bit,* etc.

Direct attention to the capital **B** in *Bill* and point out that the capital letter means that the word is a name (proper noun).

The last line of the chart shows the short-vowel sound at the beginning of a word.
Say:

Listen to the ĭ sound **(ih)** at the beginning of these words. Point to the line and read *ĭ, if, it, is, in, ill, inn.*

Sight Words

> **Note**
> Sight words do not follow the sound rules; students must memorize them. You might help your class develop memory-aid skills (e.g., mnemonic verse, pictures, sentences). Refer to *Appendix B: Sight Words Grouped by Vowel Sounds* (page 177). Although the sight words do not follow the vowel-sound rules students have learned so far, they still fall into groups having the sounds of long, short, or other vowels.

Say:

The words on the right side of the page are sight words. Point to the column headed Sight Words.

Say:

The words *live* and *give* sound like the words on the chart, but they do not follow the spelling rules. You can hear the ĭ inside these words, but they have an **e** at the end that the sound words do not have. (Point to the chart.) Write *live* and *give* on the board and have students practice saying them, with you and without you.

Call attention to the **qu** sound and words and the **qu** in the Sight Words column.
Say:

In the English language, the letter **q** is always followed by the letter **u**. Remember that **q** and **u** go together.

Point to *The, the* at the bottom of the column. (You might want to write *The, the* on the board.) Say *the* **(thuh)** and have the class repeat it a few times. Tell them they will work with *the* later in this chapter.

Words

How to Use the *Words* Section
(for example, see page 37)
Instructional Sequence

1. Students listen to the ĭ sound in sample words as you read some (or all) of them.

2. *Read*: Students read one word or a group of words at a time. Remind them to listen to the ĭ sound in each word.

3. *Write*: Students write each word.

4. *Listen and write*: Students write each word as you say it in fixed and/or mixed order.

Read: (See "How to Use the *Read* Section" on page 10 of this manual for suggestions.) Read examples to the class. Remind students to listen to the ĭ sound in each word. Read the words with the class, having them listen, then repeat them as a class and individually. Have the class read the words as you listen. If appropriate, have individuals read one or more words.

Write: See "How to Use the *Write* Section" on pages 10–11 of this manual for suggestions.

Listen and write: See "How to Use the *Listen and write* Section" on pages 11–12 of this manual for suggestions.

Read, Circle, Write

How to Use the *Read, Circle, Write* Section
(for example, see page 38)
Instructional Sequence

1. *Read*: Students read a phrase with the ĭ sound.

2. *Circle*: Students identify and circle the picture (one of two) that matches the phrase.

3. *Write*: Students write the phrase.

4. (Optional) Students *Listen and write* the phrase.

> **Note**
> This lesson measures comprehension, as well as being a reading and writing exercise.

Explain to students that they will read a phrase, circle the correct picture, then write the phrase. (Consider doing the first item with the class.) You may want to read the eight phrases with the class before students work independently.

Optional: You might want to ask students to close their books and write the phrases on a separate piece of paper, as you dictate them in fixed and/or mixed order.

Special Sounds

How to Use the *Special Sounds* Section
(for example, see page 39: *th, Th*)
Instructional Sequence

1. Students learn that **t** and **h** together make one new sound—*th*.

2. Students compare and contrast *t, h,* and *th*.

3. Students read and write eight words beginning or ending with **th**.

4. Students practice saying *the* and *with*.

5. Students listen to and write eight words beginning or ending with **th**.

Teaching Strategy Suggestions

Read: Pronounce *thuh* and have the class pronounce this sound with you. Repeat often throughout the lesson.

Compare **th** with **t** and **h** individually. At some point in this lesson, you may want to have students refer to the *Alphabet* section for **t** (page 27) and **h** (page 15) so they can review what they have accomplished and reinforce what they are learning.

Compare the sounds *th* (with throat, as in *the*) and *th* (no throat, as in *with*). Write *the* and *with* on the board and point to each word as the appropriate sound is made. This will help students concentrate on the words.

Remind students that they know the short-vowel sound $\breve{e}$ and $\breve{a}$ (as well as $\breve{\i}$) and can read *then, them, this, than, that, with, thin*. As reinforcement, ask them to refer to the *Alphabet* section for **a** (page 8) and **e** (page 16).
Say:

The *(thuh)* is an exception. This sight word doesn't follow the sound rules for the vowel.

Write: Do each section of this lesson as a complete unit, so students build their skills step by step. For example:

1. Sounds: *Read, Write, Listen and write*

2. Compare: *Read, Write, Listen and write* (**th, t, h**)

3. Words: *Read, Write, Listen and write* (**th** at the beginning and end of a word)

Encourage students to say the sounds and words quietly aloud as they write. Circulate around the room to provide assistance.

Listen and write: See "How to Use the *Listen and write* Section" on pages 11–12 of this manual for suggestions.

Special Skill

How to Use the *Special Skill* Section
(for example, see Chapter 4, page 52)

See the suggestions for "How to Use the *Special Sounds* Section" above.

Sight Words

How to Use the *Sight Words* Section
(for example, see page 40: *the, The*)

This lesson will help ensure that students can read and write *the, The*. You might want to tell students that they are learning *the, The* as a sight word now because it is used so often in English. Have them find and circle all *the, The* on one page of the local newspaper.

Note

Make sure that students understand that *the* and *The* sound exactly the same, whether capital or lowercase.

Instructional Sequence

1. Students will read and write *the* and *The* alone.

2. Students will read and write *the* and *The* in context (phrases and sentences).

3. Students will listen to and write phrases and sentences containing *the, The.*

When students are ready to read the sentences on this page, explain that the "dot" at the end of a sentence is called a period, and that it signals the end of a complete sentence. Tell them that they will have practice with this end mark as well as with others (question mark and exclamation point).

Sentences: Statements

How to Use the *Sentences: Statements* Section
(for example, see pages 41–42)

This lesson focuses on integrating the language information students have learned. To achieve and check comprehension, the lesson concentrates on reading and writing complete sentences, using the words learned on page 37, the main ideas learned on page 38, and the special sounds and sight words (**th**) on pages 39 and 40.

Instructional Sequence

1. Students read complete sentences.

2. Students write complete sentences.

3. Students listen to and write complete sentences.

Read and *Write*: See pages 10–11 of this manual for suggestions.
Listen and write: (See pages 11–12 of this manual for suggestions.) If appropriate for your class, dictate new sentences with the same words, for example:

1. The big pig is in the pit.	4. Bill hid the mitt in the tin.
2. Miss Kim is in the mill.	5. The thin kid did win.
3. Jill bit the fig.	6. Fill the rig with tins.

As another individual activity, a student may "illustrate" any of the sentences. This can be done on the board, so others in the class can share ideas. (This kind of interpretation can help you evaluate your students' comprehension.)

Sentences: Questions

How to Use the *Sentences: Questions* Section
(for example, see pages 43–44)

Explain that this lesson is similar to *Sentences: Statements*, but that these sentences ask questions. Point out that each one has a question mark (?) at the end. Say:

The question mark shows that a question is being asked.

Explain:

Each of the questions you will be reading will begin with *Did, Will,* or *Is.* You might want to write these words on the board and point out that each contains the short *ĭ* sound they have learned in this chapter.

Stories

How to Use the *Stories*

Objectives
• To use the phonetic elements and sight words learned so far in a meaningful context

• To give students a sense of accomplishment

The story brings together all of the skills learned in the chapter and provides a tangible achievement for each student. Point out this fact as often as possible, emphasizing that students can read the stories because they have already learned the phonetic elements from which they are built.

Phonetic Specifications
Each story emphasizes sounds and words presented in that chapter, and includes sounds from previous chapters.

Themes
The stories expose students to a wide scope of topics and technical information. In addition, they may be able to identify with some of the main characters. The stories in Book One cover the following themes:

Story 1: In the Mill (page 45)
   Theme: The experiences of a father and son living and working in a gristmill.

Story 2: The Tan Hats (page 62)
   Theme: A woman and a man who are friends are returning in a van from shopping for hats. They have a cat who is a little too interested in what they purchased.

Story 3: The Cab and the Big Van (page 72)
   Theme: Two pals, both skilled drivers, are racing in a demolition derby. They create a lot of action for the crowd and for themselves.

Story 4: Roz and the Doll (page 83)
   Theme: A little girl's doll is ripped by her pet dog. Mother disciplines the dog, repairs the doll, and soothes and reassures her daughter.

Story 5: A Job with Logs (pages 93–94)
   Theme: Some experiences of a lumberjack who works in a sawmill and in the woods—what he does on the job and after work, when he is joined by a friend.

Story 6: The Bus (page 102)
   Theme: A bus driver contends with annoying passengers, rush-hour traffic, and a mishap to his bus. He manages to do all this while remaining relatively calm.

Story 7: The Job at the Gull Inn (page 115)
   Theme: A man has a job as a waiter at a family-style inn. The story tells how he deals effectively with many tasks at work, a nagging boss, and the demands of the customers.

Story 8: Beth and Her Red Hen (pages 126–127)
> *Theme:* Beth, a woman who has a farm, decides to sell a hen that doesn't produce eggs. She takes a no-nonsense approach to earning a living at her egg business. She also knows the difference between a pet and a business investment.

Story 9: Did Mom, Dad, and the Kids Have Fun? (pages 139–141)
> *Theme:* A day in the life of a family. The family decides to go shopping to take advantage of a sale. They go in a van to the Jet Set, a major department store, and buy household items and clothing. The family then goes out to eat. They discuss the day and the food.

Note

Before your class starts to read each *Story,* you may want to have students number the paragraphs in the right margin in their books. (Refer to *Chapter 12: Numbers,* if necessary.) Since the discussion questions provided in this manual are numbered by paragraph, this will enable you to help students find the answers. Explain that a paragraph is made up of one or more sentences about one idea or subject. Point out the indentation that marks each new paragraph. You might want to tell students that in some printed material paragraphs are not indented, but instead are set off by extra space between them.

Instructional Sequence

1. *Read aloud in class.* Students may prepare ahead of class by reading silently or aloud to themselves at home, but this is not required. Remind them to look and listen for the sounds and words they have just learned. Start chain reading. Indicate the order you want to follow and have each student read a sentence in turn. If students' attention wanders, call on them in random order. Not knowing when they will be called on will encourage them to follow along as the reading progresses.

2. *Ask questions as the class reads to ensure comprehension.* The stories are adult-oriented; try to relate them to students' lives by asking such questions as: *Have you ever done this? Do you know anyone who has? How did you feel about it? What do you recommend?*

Point out the work-related vocabulary; there is a surprising amount of technical vocabulary available to students. Emphasize how much they can already read and comprehend, no matter what level they are at.

Ask questions such as the following. (These questions refer to the story "In the Mill" on page 45.)

Paragraph 1: What is a mill? Who is Jim? Who is Kim? What is a "kid"? Who will live in the mill?

Paragraph 2: Who will fix the mill? Who will fix the rig? What is a rig? *(a big truck)* Is Kim a big kid? What does this mean? (Kid *also means a baby goat—but not here.)*

Paragraph 3: Who got the pig? Where will the pig live? What will the pig do in the hill? Does the pig make any sound? If so, what is it? If the pig hides, who will miss it?

Paragraph 4: What happened to Jim? What is a pill? Do you think Jim and Kim are working hard at the mill? How can you tell?

After reading the entire story, lead a discussion about the theme. You might want to ask if anyone has ever seen a gristmill.

During the discussion questions, you may want to introduce important vocabulary that is beyond the phonetic scope of the lesson. You can explain that it will be taught in future lessons. For example: Story 5, Chapter 7, tells about a man who is a *lumberjack* (the multisyllabic word and the *ck* sound are taught in Book Two). Although students may not be able to read the name of the occupation yet, they can still read about its characteristics.

3. *Complete the Write section.* Use this section either as writing practice for students or as a *Listen and write* activity. If necessary, provide students with additional paper so that they have as much practice as possible.

4. *Optional Skill Reinforcement:* Have students underline in the story specific sounds from the emphasized list that you think they need help with, either before or after they read. If some students seem overwhelmed, it is helpful to do this before the reading to reinforce the idea that they know the sounds in the passage. It is important that reading the stories should be fun. Do not make it tedious.

5. *Optional Class Activities:*

   a. Use the stories as a play and have students take roles and act out parts.

   b. If possible, bring in some of the items mentioned in the stories (a bag of stone-ground flower for Story 1 or some hats for Story 4), or draw some items on the board, such as a dog or a doll for Story 6.

   c. Students may want to draw their interpretation of a particular story.

   d. You and the class may visit the workplaces identified in the stories and identify the vocabulary there.

Bonus

How to Use the *Bonus* Section
(for example, see page 46)

The *Bonus* page uses the same vocabulary as the sentences and the story, but the sentence structure is more advanced. The sentences on this page use introductory and conditional clauses. You can use the *Bonus* page as an additional activity for advanced students. It is not required that all students complete this page; omit it for the time being if it seems too difficult for your class. You can come back to it at a more appropriate time.

How to Use the Review Chapters

Objective

To review, contrast, and clarify the differences between the short vowel sounds learned so far

Explain that these distinctions are important because different vowel sounds make different words. You might want to write these examples on the board:

pin	pan	tin	tan	fit	fat
pit	pat	sit	sat	big	bag

Encourage students to enunciate clearly when they speak and to listen carefully for the differences between vowels when others speak.

Below is a discussion of how to use each section of a review chapter. *Chapter 5: Review of the ă and ĭ Sounds* is used as the example.

Sounds

How to Use the *Sounds* Section
(for example, see pages 64–65)

Review the vowel sounds alone on the top line *(ă, ĭ)*. Refer back to the *Sounds* page for each vowel, if necessary. Then read the consonants with the vowel sounds *(bă, bĭ)*. Have students write each sound once or twice in the space provided.

Read: First, read across, left to right *(bă, bĭ; că; dă, dĭ)*. Emphasize that while the consonant remains the same, the vowel sound changes. If you think your students need more practice with one vowel sound, read down the columns *(bă, că, dă, etc.)* after you have read across all of them.

> **Note**
> Sound spaces that have dashes indicate that this sound is not common in English or will be taught in Book Two or Three.

Listen and write: See "How to Use the *Listen and write* Section" on pages 11–12 of this manual for suggestions.

In the *Review* chapters, *Listen and write* is indicated as fixed order and mixed order (for example, see page 65). *Fixed order* means to dictate the sounds or words across the page, left to right, following the indicated vowel at the top of the column. For example, on page 65, the fixed order columns are headed *ă* and *ĭ*. Therefore, dictate sounds in *pairs (bă, bĭ; lă, lĭ; mă, mĭ)*. You can also vary the consonants *(bă, lĭ; lă, mĭ; ră, sĭ)*. For example, you can do three lines of matched consonants and three lines of varied consonants. *Mixed order* columns do not have vowel headers. Dictate sounds in any combination you want. For example: *bĭ, să; rĭ, mĭ; lă, tă; nĭ, pă.*

First, dictate the sounds (vowels with consonants) in **fixed order.** For example, *bă, bĭ; că; dă, dĭ.* Tell students to write the sound in the correct column under the matching vowel. You may want to write a few items on the board, to clarify the concept of "correct column and matching vowel." Point out the headings (*ă* and *ĭ*) and the columns where students would write *bă* and *bĭ.*

Second, dictate the sounds in **mixed order** (random order). Have students finish numbering the blank lines consecutively (see page 65). If the last numbered line is *3*, then the next column should be *4, 5,* and *6*. (Refer to *Chapter 12: Numbers,* if necessary.) Have students write the sounds in numerical order as you dictate, for example, 1. *bĭ* 2. *kĭ* 3. *vă* 4. *sĭ* 5. *tă* 6. *ră.* Dictate individual sounds, not pairs. Students write down the columns, not across the rows. As students get more skilled at *Listen and write*, you can dictate mixed order in pairs. Then they do not have to number columns, as they would write across the rows.

Sound Words

How to Use the *Sound Words* Section
(for example, see pages 66–67)

Have students read, contrast, and write the words with the *ă* and *ĭ* sounds. Follow the suggestions for "How to Use the *Sounds* Section" above.

Sight Words

How to Use the *Sight Words* Section
(for example, see page 68)

(See pages 30–31 of this manual for suggestions.)

These are the sight words taught to this point. This review offers practice to ensure that students have memorized each one.

> **Note**
> The sight words are presented with both capital and small initial letters. Stress that they are the same words and sound the same. Use the first *Write* column for initial small letter words and the second column for initial capital letter words.

Refer to *Appendix B: Sight Words Grouped by Vowel Sounds* (page 177). Even though the sight words do not follow the rules students have learned so far, they still fall into groups having the sounds of short, long, or other vowels.

Listen and write: Dictate the sight words, preferably in mixed order. However, if your students are not confident of their ability, dictate in fixed order.

Sentences: Statements

Sentences: Questions

How to Use the *Sentences: Statements* and *Sentences: Questions* Sections
(for example, see pages 69–71)

This sentence review uses the sound words and sight words from Chapters 4 and 5. The lesson emphasizes both $\breve{a}$ and $\breve{i}$ sounds, compared and contrasted. Students read and write the sentences, and indicate the different vowels in each sentence.

For additional activities, students can underline one particular vowel (**a**), circle another (**i**), and/or box the sight words.

Listen and write: See "How to Use the *Listen and write* Section" on pages 11–12 of this manual for suggestions.

Select and dictate sentences from pages 69 and 70, using any order. You can make up sentences, using the previously learned sound words and sight words.

If the sentences are too difficult at first, start with phrases. Use as much or as little of the available space on the page as appropriate for the ability and interest of your class.

Stories

How to Use the *Stories*
(for example, see page 72)

Emphasize the different vowel sounds used together here.
Ask such questions as:

Paragraph 1: What kind of car does Dan have? What is inside? Can he live in it?

Paragraph 2: What is Dan's pal's name? What kind of car does Bill have?

Paragraph 3: Who has a hat? Who has a cap?

Paragraph 4: Where do they race? Who will fix the van if it is hit? Who will fix the cab if it is hit?

Paragraph 5: Who won? Who is mad? Why did Dan bite his lip?

For additional suggestions see "How to Use the Stories" on pages 32–34 of this manual.

Chapter 3: Words with the *ĭ* Sound

See "How to Use the Vowel Chapters" on pages 26–34 of this manual. This chapter is used as the example there.

Chapter 4: Words with the *ă* Sound

See "How to Use the Vowel Chapters" on pages 26–34 of this manual. Only variations and exceptions to presentation, instructional sequences, or teaching strategy suggestions given there will be noted in this section.

Objective

To read and write words, sentences, and a story with the short-vowel sound *ă* and related sight words.

Page 47

The short-vowel sound *ă*

Say:

This is *ă* as in *apple*.   Point to the picture at the top of the page. (You might want to draw an apple on the board or bring one to class and pass it around the room.)

Sounds

Read: Read part of the first line to the class, emphasizing the short-vowel *ă* sound. For example: *bă, că, dă* . . . .

> **Note**
> Omitted from the chart are *kă* and *wă* sounds: *kă* is not common (*că* is common), and *wă* usually has a special sound as in *watch* (Book Three).

Sounds and Words

Say:

The words on the right side of the page are sight words. (Point to the column headed **Sight Words.**)

Say:

The word *have* sounds like the words on the chart. You can hear the *ă* inside it. The only difference is that *have* has a silent **e** at the end.

Write *have* on the board and have students practice saying it with you and without you. (As reinforcement, you may want to go back to page 8 in the student text, where the *ă* sound was introduced.)

Point out the sight words at the bottom of the column (*I, you, they, we, he, she, be, are, A/a*). Say each word and have students repeat after you. Tell them they will be working with these sight words later in this chapter.

Have students pay particular attention to **A/a**. Explain that it sounds like **uh** whether it is capital or lowercase.

Page 50 ## Sentences

Point out that the sentences correspond to the words on page 48 and the phrases and pictures on page 49.)

Page 51 ## Sight Word: *a/A*

Remind students that *a/A* sounds like **uh.** Practice this sound with them, then ask each student to pronounce it. Compare the **uh** sound of **a/A** with the short-vowel *ă* found in *bag, hat, map, man, sat, . . .*

Pages 52–53 ## Special Skill: Compare *a/An*

The emphasis on this skill page is to become aware of how *a/an* are used. Point out that *a* precedes a consonant and *an* precedes a vowel. Call attention to the exceptions (Special Cases) of **u, y, h.** This is a good time to explain that the vowels of the English alphabet are **a, e, i, o, u** (and sometimes **y**) and that the rest of the letters are consonants. (These will be studied in detail in Book Two.)

Have students read all the words with *a* and *an* that they know, then write these phrases in the space provided.

Students may not know some of the example words. Explain that they will be learning them later in this book or in Books Two and Three. (You may want to have them look at the *Alphabet* pages in their text, where some of these words are illustrated.) Students don't have to learn the words here. They are looking only for the relationship between *a/an* and the initial letter of the word.

If your group is advanced (or you have some students who want more of a challenge) review this section in more detail, discussing and comparing the differences. If you want, all the students can use this section to practice their writing skills.

Dictate words appropriate to this lesson for the *Listen and write,* emphasizing the use of *a* or *an.* Take them from pages 52 and 53 and use them in random order.

Write a or an: Students will fill in the blank before each word with *a* or *an,* based on the spelling or sound of the word. You can use this section as a test of comprehension, as an oral activity (with students completing the items later), or a class practice after you complete two items on the board. Check students' answers and correct their mistakes. Point out that the correct form is given on page 52.

Answers:

1. a mill	5. a bin	9. an inch
2. a wig	6. an ax	10. a ham
3. a rat	7. an inn	11. an herb
4. a ring	8. an umbrella	12. a union

Page 54 ## Special Skill: Plurals

Say:

An **s** at the end of an already complete word means "more than one" (plural).

Point out the differences between the single examples and the plural examples in the text. Find other examples in the room, such as two students (point to one student, then to two or more students); one shoe, two shoes (use your own shoes as the example); one book, two or more books; one pencil, two or more pencils. Emphasize the sound of *s* or *z* at the end of these words.

Say:

Some plurals do not have an **s** at the end.

Point out one man and one woman in the class, then two men and two women, emphasizing the difference in pronunciation. Point to one foot (your own), then to both feet. Explain that the inside letter or letters change and that no **s** is added to the plural words. Tell students that they will be learning these skills in Books Two and Three.

Page 55   ## Special Skill: Compare *has*/*have*

Say:

Has is the singular verb and is used with one person or thing. *Have* is the plural verb and is used with more than one person or thing.

Emphasize that in English, verbs relate to the number of people or things doing the action, not to whether they are male or female. As examples, point to the first two illustrations on page 55. Be sure that everyone understands that Nan is a woman and Vin is a man, then explain that the only difference in the sentences is the name (proper noun) of the person.

Go on to explain that *have* is used with plural nouns in any combination of males, females, and males and females. Point out the examples in the text.

Pages 56–57   ## Special Skill: The Verb *to be* (Present Tense)

> **Note**
> Extra time spent on this grammar lesson will be well worth the effort. Understanding how to use the verb *to be* will help students build on other lessons and increase their self-esteem.

Say:

Some of the sounds and words on this page are exceptions to what you have learned so far. You will have to memorize them.

(You might want to advise students to put a paper clip on this page so that they can refer to the Singular and Plural information box.)

Direct attention to the Sight Words listed in the information box. Point to the two columns and explain that these phrases are used often in speaking, reading, and writing. Say each phrase and point to a "definition." For example, say:

I am (point to yourself; add a common action, such as *walking);*

You are (point to a student; add *sitting, standing*);

He is (point to a male student; add an easy-to-understand action);

She is (point to a female student; add an easy-to-understand action).

Follow the same pattern for the Plural list. Explain that *you are* is used for both singular and plural, and that *it* always refers to things, not to people.

Read: When students are ready, have them read the phrases as a class, first with you, then without you, then individually. You may want to write the list on the board.

Write: Encourage students to say each phrase quietly aloud as they write it.

Listen and write: Dictate each phrase (have students cover the top half of the page). Depending on the achievement of the class, dictate the list in fixed order or in mixed order.

Page 57

Complete with a form of *to be*

Before students work on this page, review the basic information about *to be*. If this strategy works well with your class, you may also want to provide more examples of usage and ask students to role-play the actions. For example:

He is a man. She is standing. I am a teacher. You are students. We are in the classroom. They are writing on the board. You are listening. We are opening/closing the books.

Complete: You can use these sections in many ways—as a test; as a small-group activity, with students working in teams of three or four; or as additional individual practice. Check students' answers and correct their mistakes.

Part I Answers:

1. be	5. is	1. to	5. it
2. am	6. are	2. I	6. we
3. is	7. are	3. he	7. you
4. is	8. are	4. she	8. they

Part II Answers:

1. I am on a bus.	5. We are at the mill.
2. He is a man.	6. You are in the cab.
3. She is a mom.	7. They are cats.
4. It is a dog.	8. They are tots.

If you think it might be helpful, display pictures of the items mentioned in the sentences.

Listen and write: Select and dictate any number or combination of the phrases and sentences, using either fixed order or mixed order.

Pages 58–59

Sentences: Statements

Pages 60–61

Sentences: Questions

These lessons focus on integrating the language information students have learned so far—the sounds, words, sight words, and grammar in Chapter 4 (pages 47–57).

Page 62   **Story 2: The Tan Hats**
Ask questions such as:

Paragraph 1: Is Nan a man or a woman? What does she have? Is Sam a man or a woman? What does he have? What is a hat? What color is it? What is a tag? What is a tax?

Paragraph 2: Where are the hats? Where are the bags?

Paragraph 3: What sat in the van? Why?

Paragraph 4: What did the cat do to the hats?

Paragraph 5: What did the cat do? What will Sam and Nan do?

Chapter 5: Review of the ă and ĭ Sounds

See "How to Use the Review Chapters" on pages 34–36 of this manual. This chapter is used as the example there.

Chapter 6: Words with the ŏ Sound

See "How to Use the Vowel Chapters" on pages 26–34 of this manual. Only variations and exceptions to presentation, instructional sequence, or teaching strategy suggestions given there will be noted in this lesson.

Objective

To read and write words, sentences, and a story with the short-vowel sound ŏ and related sight words

Page 73   **The short-vowel sound ŏ**
Say:

This is **ŏ** as in *octopus*.   Point to the picture at the top of the page.

Sounds
Read: Read part of the first line to the class, emphasizing the short-vowel sound ŏ. For example **bŏ, cŏ, dŏ** . . . .

Sounds and Words
See pages 27–28 of this manual. Use the same teaching strategy that you used for **ă.**
　Read: **buh, bŏ, bob, Bob,** etc.

> **Note**
> In both the *Sounds* and *Sounds and Words* charts, read the ŏ sound as in *octopus* for **dŏ, tŏ, gŏ, nŏ, sŏ.** These will be the starting sounds of the words on the chart. Emphasize that the sight words on the right side of page 73 have different sounds and that students will have to memorize them. They will be taught in the following pages of this chapter.

　Sight Words: Explain that *do* and *to* rhyme; *go, no,* and *so* rhyme (with the long-vowel sound ō) and do not have the short-vowel sound ŏ as in *octopus*.

Page 76   **Sentences**

These sentences use the comprehension concepts of *Read, Circle, Write*, page 75.

Page 77   **Sight Word: *to, To***

Practice the sight word *to*, emphasizing the difference between *to* and the sound *tŏ* as in *top, Tom, tot*. Say:

The sight word *to* sounds like the number *two*.

Page 78   **Sight Word: *do***

Practice the sight word *do*, emphasizing the difference between the word *do* and the sound *dŏ* as in *dog, doll, Don*.

Pages 79–80   **Sentences: Statements**

Pages 81–82   **Sentences: Questions**

These lessons focus on integrating language information students have learned so far—the sounds, words, sight words, and grammar in Chapter 6.

Call attention to the new question word *Do*. Point out how many question words students know (see list, top of page 81).

Point out that quotation marks ("/") go before and after the exact words a person speaks. Also note the use of exclamation points (!), and explain that this punctuation mark is used to indicate strong feelings and surprise.

Page 83   **Story 4: Roz and the Doll**

Ask questions such as:

Paragraph 1: Is Roz a child or an adult? What toy does Roz have? What's the doll's name? Where is the doll? Where is the box?

Paragraph 2: Does Roz have a pet? Is it a cat or a dog? What is its name? Is the pet big?

Paragraph 3: What did Tom do? With the box? With the doll?

Paragraph 4: How does Roz feel? What did Mom do? What did Mom say to Tom? What did Tom do? How does Tom feel? Do you think the dog will behave now?

Paragraph 5: Who will fix the doll? What did Mom do and say to Roz?

Chapter 7: Review of the *ă*, *ĭ*, and *ŏ* Sounds

See "How to Use the Review Chapters" on pages 34–36 of this manual. Only variations and additions to the format given there will be noted in this section.

Objectives

To review, contrast, and clarify the differences between the short-vowel sounds *ă, ĭ, ŏ*

Explain that these distinctions are important because different vowel sounds make different words. You might want to write *pat, pit, pot* on the board as examples. Encourage students to enunciate clearly when they speak and to listen carefully for the differences when others speak.

Pages 93–94   Story 5: A Job with Logs

Ask questions such as:

Paragraph 1: Where is Ron's job? What does Ron do on his job? What tool does Ron use?

Paragraph 2: What is a bog? What is a rig? *(a big truck)* Where did Ron go in his rig? What tools did Ron take with him? What is on the logs? Will the moss rot the logs? What will Ron do with his ax? Why?

Paragraph 3: What happened at the dam? What is a log jam? Who will fix it? Tell how.

Paragraph 4: Where did Ron put the logs? What did Ron's boss do? Does Ron like his job? How do you know?

Paragraph 5: Where is Ron at six? What is the name of his pal? Is Ron's pal a man or a woman? (Explain that Ron's pal could be either a man or a woman, since *Pat* is a name used by both males and females.) What are the foods that Ron and Pat have? Do you think the pals like animals? How do you know?

Paragraph 6: After Ron and Pat eat, what do they do? What does *gab* mean?

Chapter 8: Words with the *ŭ* Sound

See "How to Use the Vowel Chapters" on pages 26–34 of this manual. Only variations and exceptions to presentation, instructional sequences, and teaching strategy suggestions given there will be noted in this section.

Objective

To read and write words, sentences, and a story with the short-vowel sound *ŭ* and related sight words

Page 95   The short-vowel sound *ŭ*

Say:

This is *ŭ* as in *umbrella*.   Point to the picture at the top of the page. If you have an umbrella available, show it to the class.

Sounds
Read: Read part of the first line to the class, emphasizing the short-vowel *ŭ* sound. For example: **bŭ, cŭ, dŭ** . . . .

Sounds and Words
Read: **buh,** bud, but, etc.

Sight Words: Point out the sight words that have the *ŭ* sound of *umbrella: come, some, son, of.* Then call attention to the sight words that have a different sound of **u:** *full, pull, put.* Remind students that they must memorize these words.

Pages 98–99   Sentences: Statements

Pages 100–101   Sentences: Questions

These pages emphasize words with the *ŭ* sound and related sight words from pages 95–96. Sentences 1 through 8 on page 98 also incorporate the comprehension concepts of *Read, Circle, Write* (page 97).

Listen and write: Dictate whole or partial sentences in fixed or random order.

Page 102   Story 6: The Bus

Ask such questions as:

Paragraph 1: What does Judd do for a living? Does he get up early in the morning? Is Judd's job dull?

Paragraph 2: Where is Judd running? What does Judd do when he gets to his bus? Will Judd stop at a gas station? Why or why not?

Paragraph 3: Who got on the bus? What is a bus pass? (If you don't have this prepaid system in your area, explain that a bus pass is a plastic identification card that allows passengers to "show and go" on public transportation. Passengers buy a monthly pass, usually at a savings over the daily rate.)

Paragraph 4: Who else got on the bus? Was he alone? What did the kid do? How did the man feel? What did the man do? What did Judd do? Why?

Paragraph 5: What did the man do after he got off the bus?

Paragraph 6: What did the cab do? What happened to the bus? How did Judd feel?

Paragraph 7: Did the big man help? How? (van, here = tow truck, Book Three) What happened to the bus? How does Judd feel now?

Paragraph 8: Do you think Judd likes his job?

Use the *Write* section to write and / or *Listen and write* sentences or phrases from the story.

Chapter 9: Review of the *ă*, *ĭ*, *ŏ*, and *ŭ* Sounds

See "How to Use the Review Chapters" on pages 34–36 of this manual. Only variations and additions to the format given there will be noted in this section.

Objective

To review, contrast, and clarify the differences between the short-vowel sounds *ă*, *ĭ*, *ŏ*, and *ŭ*

Explain that these distinctions are important because different vowel sounds make different words. You might want to write *bag, big, bog, bug* on the board as examples.

Encourage students to enunciate clearly when they speak, and to listen carefully for the differences when others speak.

Pages 107–108   Sound Words

Read and contrast words with the *ă, ĭ, ŏ, ŭ* vowel sounds.

Pages 109–111   Sight Words

For the *Listen and write* sections on page 111, dictate any number of words in any order. Use only the sight words at the top of the page. Emphasize that students must memorize the sight words because they do not follow the sound rules. Have them finish numbering the columns on page 111, top to bottom (11–20, 21–30, 31–40).

Dictate both sight and sound words at the bottom half of page 111. Have students finish numbering the columns first.

Page 112   Sentences: Statements

Pages 113–114   Sentences: Questions

These sentences focus on integrating the language information students have learned so far—the sound words, sight words, and grammar from Chapters 3 through 8.

Emphasize, compare, and contrast the *ă, ĭ, ŏ,* and *ŭ* sounds. For example: contrast vowels: *Bob, bit, gum, bag* (from Statement 1); contrast beginning consonants: *not, rot* (from Statement 3).

Listen and write: Dictate sentences or phrases from pages 112–113 in any order.

Page 115   Story 7: The Job at the Gull Inn

Ask questions such as:

Paragraph 1: What is an inn? *(restaurant and hotel, Book Three)* What is a gull? What does Kim do for a living? *(waiter, Book Three)* Where does Kim live? How does Kim dress for his job? Do you think Kim earns much? Why? What is a tip?

Paragraph 2: List the tasks Kim does at the inn. Do you think he's skilled at his work? *(yes)* Why? *(He can have a lot of tips, paragraph 1; reward for good service.)*

Paragraph 3: Who were Kim's customers? How many people? List what they wanted to eat. What is a bill? What are the three things Kim did on the bill? Do you think the customers liked Kim and thought he did a good job? Why?

Paragraph 4: What is Kim's boss like? Will Kim quit his job? Why or why not?

Chapter 10: Words with the *ĕ* Sound

See "How to Use the Vowel Chapters" on pages 26–34 of this manual. Only variations and exceptions to presentation, instructional sequence, and teaching strategy suggestions given there will be noted in this section.

The emphasis in this chapter is on the short-vowel sound *ĕ*. The *ĕ* sound is taught last because it is frequently the most difficult short-vowel sound to master.

Objectives

To read and write words, sentences, and a story with the short-vowel sound *ĕ* and related sight words.

Page 117

The short-vowel sound *ĕ*

Say:

This is *ĕ* as in *egg*.   Point to the picture at the top of the page.

Sounds
Read: Read the first line to the class, emphasizing the short-vowel *ĕ* sound as in *egg*. It is important to emphasize the sounds *bĕ, hĕ, mĕ, wĕ* as **beh, heh, meh, weh,** and not pronounce them as the sight words on that page.

Sounds and Words
Go over the sounds *bĕ, hĕ, mĕ, wĕ* as **beh, heh, meh, weh.**

> **Note**
> The *ce* sound and *ce* words (such as *cell*) are omitted from this lesson because **c** has the soft sound of **s** before **e**. In this book, **c** is used only with its hard sound of **k**. The soft sound of **c** is taught in Book 2, Chapter 3, where *ce* and *ci* are featured as special sounds.

   Sight words: Help students differentiate the sight words *be, he, me, we, she* from the short-vowel sound of *eh*. Make sure they understand that *said* sounds like *eh* but is spelled differently.

Page 120

Sight Words: He/he, She/she, Me/me, We/we, Be/be
(See text pages 117–118.)
Contrast the sight words *he, she, me, we, be* with the starting sound *hĕ (heh), mĕ (meh), wĕ (weh), bĕ (beh).*

Page 121

Sight Words: *her/Her*
Contrast the sight words *his* and *her*. Make sure everyone understands that *her* is female and *his* is male. For example: Sentence 1: *Nan* leads to Sentence 2: *her* dog; Sentence 5: *her* mom; and Sentence 6: *her* dad (emphasize that *her* agrees with the subject, Nan, not the object, dad). Sentence 3: *Tim* leads to Sentence 4: *his* dog; Sentence 7: *his* mom (emphasize that *his* agrees with the subject, Tim, not the object, mom); and Sentence 8: *his* dad.

Pages 122–123

Sentences: Statements
The sentences are *not* related to the *Read, Circle, Write* on page 119, although a few have similar phrases.

Pages 124–125

Sentences: Questions and Answers
Explain that in each pair of sentences, the first is a question, the second an answer to the question.

Pages 126–127

Story 8: Beth and Her Red Hen
Ask questions such as:

Paragraph 1: What does Beth have? How many? Are Beth's hens pets to her? Why or why not? What does Beth do with the eggs?

Paragraph 2: What does Beth think of her red hen? Why? What will she do with the hen?

Paragraph 3: Where will she sell the hen? What does Beth think will happen to the hen at the inn? *("Cook" it, Book Three)*

Paragraph 4: How does she carry the hen to the inn? What is Rex? Does Beth say anything to Rex? What did she say and how do you know? (Remind students about quotation marks.)

Paragraph 5: At the inn, what does Rex do? What does the hen do? What does Beth do? How does Beth get the hen to come back to her?

Paragraph 6: What do Jeff and Ted plan to do with the red hen? Who gives whom "ten big bills"? (Discuss what "ten big bills" might mean. *[money? $10? $100? $1000?]*) How much is a hen worth?

Paragraph 7: What is Beth doing? How does she feel? What does "had had it" mean? (See Appendix C: Idioms.) At the end, what has Beth got? What do Jeff and Ted have?

Use the *Write* section to write and/or *Listen and write.*

Chapter 11: Review of the *ă, ĕ, ĭ, ŏ,* and *ŭ* Sounds

See "How to Use the Review Chapters" on pages 34–36 of this manual. Only variations and additions to the format given there will be noted in this section.

Pages 139–141

Story 9: Did Mom, Dad, and the Kids Have Fun?

At this point in the text, the story is fairly complex. The vocabulary covers a range of common words and experiences. Direct attention to the subheads in the story. Explain that they indicate a change of scene and action.

> **Note**
> *Numbering the paragraphs:* Point out that this story has twenty-one paragraphs. Explain that some are only one sentence because they represent one person's speech, and each speaker's words are set off in a separate paragraph. Remind students to look for the indentations that mark the beginning of each paragraph.

The story is divided into three sections by subheads:

1. *The Big Ad* (paragraphs 1–6)

2. *At the Jet Set* (paragraphs 7–14)

3. *At the Gull Inn* (paragraphs 15–21)

Ask questions such as:

The Big Ad

Paragraph 1: What is an ad? Where did they read the ad? *(probably in a newspaper)*

> **Note**
> Distribute a few department store ads from the local newspaper for students to look over and discuss. This will help them grasp the concepts in the story.

Paragraph 2: What does Mom plan to do?

Paragraph 3: What does Dad plan to do?

Paragraph 4: What do Mom and Dad do?

Paragraph 5: What do the kids want to do? How do they travel?

Paragraph 6: How does Dad say they will go?

At the Jet Set

Paragraph 7: What is the Jet Set? (It gets its name from the expression that refers to people who like to travel fast [by jet], like to buy expensive things, and have lots of money to spend.) What did they get at the store?

Paragraph 8: What did Mom and the kids get? What did Dad and the kids get?

Paragraph 9: What did Ben get? What color is it? What did Ann try on? Did she get it? How did she feel? What did Dad try on? Did he get it? Why? What did Jill get?

Paragraph 10: How were the family's purchases packed?

Paragraph 11: Who will carry the big box? Who will carry the bags?

Paragraph 12: Will the van be full?

Paragraph 13: Did the family spend a lot of money?

Paragraph 14: Was it fun for the family to shop at the Jet Set?

At the Gull Inn

Paragraph 15: What does Dad ask?

Paragraph 16: What does Mom say?

Paragraph 17: Where did the family go? What did they eat?

Paragraph 18: What does Ben ask Jill?

Paragraph 19: Does Jill do it?

Paragraph 20: What else did the kids eat? What did Mom and Dad eat? Are they fat? Are they full?

Paragraph 21: Can they all get into the van? Did they have fun at the Gull Inn?

Unit Three: Life Skills

Most of the skills in Unit Three are taught as sight words. Because these skills are necessary to daily life, encourage students to memorize them at this time. They will learn the rules for spelling and pronunciation in Books Two and Three.

Teach the skills in Unit Three at any point in the book after the *Alphabet* pages. For example, you might want to teach some numbers after Chapter 3 *(ĭ)* and after Chapter 5 (review of *ă* and *ĭ*).

Chapter 12: Numbers

Page 144   ### Counting Summary Chart

Encourage students to use this chart as a reference. Have them count for practice. Emphasize families of numbers: teens, twenties, thirties, etc.

Page 145   ### Digits: 0–9

Read and write: Have students count the dots and compare the digit to the number of dots. Encourage them to memorize these numbers. Start teaching these numbers after the *Alphabet* pages. After students read the numbers, they will trace three of them, then write them.

Additional Activities

1. Dictate the numbers in fixed and mixed order.

2. Put some simple math problems on the board, none totaling more than 9. Ask students to copy them. Explain the plus (+), minus (−), multiplication/times (×), and division/divided by (÷) signs. Encourage your students to solve the math problems.

Note

If appropriate for your class, use only addition problems, but you may want to provide a few subtraction, multiplication, and division examples.

When you read a math problem, use the third-person singular verb *(is, equals)*.

For addition, say: One (plus/and) two (is/equals) three; four (plus/and) four (plus/and) zero (is/equals) eight).

$$\begin{array}{cccccc} & 1 & 3 & 9 & \overset{1}{2} & \overset{4}{4} \\ & +2 & +5 & +0 & +6 & +0 \\ \hline & 3 & 8 & 9 & 9 & 8 \end{array}$$

For subtraction, say: Eight (minus/take away) five (is/equals) three.

$$\begin{array}{ccccc} 8 & 2 & 7 & 0 & 6 \\ -5 & -1 & -3 & -0 & -4 \\ \hline 3 & 1 & 4 & 0 & 2 \end{array}$$

For multiplication, say: Three times two (is/equals) six.

$$\begin{array}{l} 3 \\ \times 2 \\ \hline 6 \end{array} \quad \text{or} \quad 3 \times 2 = 6$$

For division, say: Six divided by two (is/equals) six.

$$2\overline{)6}\,^{3} \quad \text{or} \quad 6 \div 2 = 3$$

Pages 146–151

Number Names

Call attention to the forms of the numbers: digits and words in book type, hand printing, and script. Note the hyphen in names of numbers composed of two words under one hundred.

Pages 152–153

The Calendar

Compare the calendar shown with actual calendars. Discuss how the dates and days are written across. Point out that English calendars begin the week with Sunday.

Compare and contrast the days of the week and their abbreviations. Call attention to the period at the end of each abbreviation.

Compare and contrast the months of the year and their abbreviations.

Additional Activities

1. Encourage students to keep a record of dates that are important to them (birthdays, anniversaries, holidays, etc.).

2. Provide a blank calendar form (a page with thirty-five large spaces blocked out) for each student. Help the class complete the calendar for one month. Students can then use it to fill in appointments, class hours, work hours, special trips, occasions, etc. At the end of the month, discuss the activity with the class. Did everyone learn the calendar words and numbers? Were they better able to plan their time and keep their appointments? Did they remember special dates more easily?

Pages 154–158

The Clock: Telling Time

Read the footnotes and directions on the text pages before beginning this section.

Students will need to memorize this information. Practice throughout the book, after the *Alphabet* pages, so that they can incorporate the data and continually reinforce their skills.

Explain that time can be written and pronounced in several ways. They can learn one way to speak about time, but they should be aware that they will hear and read other forms. (Standard for usage: *The Chicago Manual of Style*, The University of Chicago Press, 1982.)

Point out the two different types of clocks that are illustrated in the lesson: regular face and digital. Discuss the differences. (The face clock has a big hand, a little hand, and [sometimes] a second hand.)

Pages 159–160

Time Exercises

Encourage students to complete the sentences on page 159 according to their own personal life habits. If you prefer, use these suggestions:

2. seven thirty in the morning, 7:30 A.M.

3. five minutes to eight in the morning, 7:55 A.M.

4. eight fifteen in the morning, 8:15 A.M.

5. nine o'clock in the morning, 9:00 A.M. *or* 9 A.M.

6. noon, 12:00 m *or* 12 m

7. ten minutes after five in the afternoon, 5:10 P.M.

8. six thirty in the evening, 6:30 P.M.

9. eleven o'clock at night, 11:00 P.M. *or* 11 P.M.

Tell students to write what they would say on the top half of page 160. Some possibilities are:

2. three thirty in the afternoon

3. six fifteen in the evening

4. seven forty-five at night *or* a quarter to eight at night

5. twelve noon *or* noon

6. twelve midnight *or* midnight

7. five seventeen in the morning *or* A.M.

8. eight twenty-nine at night *or* P.M.

9. four fifty-one in the morning *or* A.M.

10. two "oh" four in the afternoon *or* four minutes after two in the afternoon

11. nine thirty-five in the morning *or* A.M. *or* twenty-five minutes to ten in the morning

Have students write the time in numbers on the bottom half of page 160:

2. 4:30 P.M.	5. 7:10 A.M.
3. 5:15 A.M.	6. 7:40 P.M.
4. 8:45 P.M.	7. 12:00 P.M. *or* 12 P.M.

Additional Activities

Students frequently develop coping mechanisms that allow them to read the time in some approximate form, but they cannot pronounce it or understand it when it is spoken. For example, they may read 3:25 as "three five," reading only the numbers on the face of the clock and not the five-minute intervals they represent. Refer to the wall clock in your classroom or to students' watches. Focus on the time the class meets, goes on break, returns from break, and is over.

Chapter 13: Colors

Pages 161–162   Students learn the color names as sight words; they can, however, sound out *red* and *tan*. Have them use markers or crayons to color in the circles.

Encourage them to see and practice color in four forms: the actual color in the circle, and the color word in book type, hand printing, and script.

Additional Activities

1. If possible, bring in swatches of cloth. Have students match/identify the colors with the color samples in their text. Point out that colors have different shades (such as light blue, sky blue, and navy blue). Some students may be willing to discuss the colors they are wearing; if any wear uniforms at work, they may want to describe them.

2. If possible, go outdoors with the class. Ask students to observe and identify the colors around them; for example, in the daytime, green grass, blue sky, white clouds; at night, black/gray sky, yellow/white stars and moon; also red brick buildings, gray concrete buildings, black tarred roadways/parking lots, orange buses, blue police cars, etc.

3. If appropriate for your class, discuss color "moods." For example, ask students if a yellow, sunny day seems more cheerful than a gray, rainy one.

Chapter 14: Personal Identification

Pages 163–164   ## Abbreviations

Students must learn these as sight words.

Explain that abbreviations are shortened forms of titles and places, but stress that they are "standardized," not randomly made up. Point out that most of these abbreviations can be found in dictionaries.

Titles

Explain that these are common titles that go with the names of people. Point out that the titles in items 5 through 9 are all *Dr.* Stress that titles are used in abbreviated form (point out the periods) with names.

Places

These common place names are used either in abbreviated form or spelled out. Sometimes U.S.A. is shown without periods—USA. Point out that the *of* in *United States of America* is dropped in the abbreviated form.

At some point in this lesson, you may want to mention the Postal System's identification system: Two-letter abbreviated state names (no period), followed by the zip (zone improvement plan) code.

Other Abbreviations

Explain that this general information is frequently used on forms of all kinds, including letterheads of companies. Remind students that they know *TV* from *Alphabet* page 27.

If appropriate for your students, you may also want to write on the board and "translate" the additional terms that follow and any others that might be relevant to their lives:

VCR = videocassette recorder
IBM = International Business Machines
corp./Corp. = corporation
NBC = National Broadcasting Company
ABC = American Broadcasting Company
SCUBA = self-contained underwater breathing apparatus

OTC = over the counter
CD = compact disk
UN = United Nations
CBS = Columbia Broadcasting System
PBS = Public Broadcasting System
PTA = Parent-Teacher Association
ASAP = as soon as possible
FYI = for your information

Additional activities

1. Students practice printing and writing the name of their state in abbreviated form, followed by the zip code (page 167).

2. Students practice printing and writing their titles, names, and addresses.

3. Work with students to decode the acronyms and abbreviations in the local newspaper. If appropriate, encourage them to bring in some they have learned at work to share with the class.

Pages 165–169   ## Answering Questions

Name, Country, Nationality, and Address
Students write in three common ways: uppercase and lowercase hand printing, all capital hand printing, "block letters" (frequently required on forms), and script (for signature). If students have a middle name and prefer to use the initial, encourage them to do so.

Have students either copy the example or write their personal information. When they finish, review their work and help them make corrections. They should then write the information again for practice.

Telephone and Social Security Numbers
Students may use the examples provided. If possible, encourage them to use their own numbers. Those who don't have social security numbers can use the numbers on their passports or other papers.

What is your job (occupation)? What do you do?
Students can use their own occupations or copy the one provided. They should write in three common ways: uppercase and lowercase hand printing, all capital hand printing (block letters), and script.

Appendices

There are three appendices, each with its own format. The skills summarized appear throughout Book One and can be used in a variety of ways:

1. To provide a review for students at the end of Book One.

2. To provide reinforcement of the skills learned, and to show students how far they have advanced. (Point out how many words and idioms they can read and understand.)

3. For *Additional Activities*. Draw from these summaries of information to:

   • generate sentences for *Listen and write*

   • provide material for additional practice

   • use as reference charts

Appendix A: Scope and Sequence Charts

These charts list the words taught in each major short-vowel chapter in the order that they are taught: *ĭ, ă, ŏ, ŭ, ĕ*. Words are grouped by parts of speech. The sight words are included.

You and your students can use these charts to form new sentences. Read down the column; have them listen for the emphasized vowel.

Appendix B: Sight Words Grouped by Vowel Sounds

This chart shows that, although sight words do not follow the rules for short-vowel words, the sounds of some of the sight words are similar to the short and long vowels taught in the *Alphabet* section (rows 1 and 2) and others (row 3). These words fall into groups that will be taught as sound families in Books Two and Three.

Appendix C: Idioms

Page 178 lists twenty common idioms that use the five short vowels and sight words taught in Book One. The definitions are given to help you explain their meanings. Do not expect students to be able to read the definitions, since they are at a higher level than the idioms themselves.

Emphasize the importance and common usage of idioms in everyday speech. Congratulate students for being able to read so many idioms.

Page 179 provides twenty sentences corresponding by number to the twenty idioms and definitions on page 178. Students can read these sentences.

On page 180, have students *Write* or, if appropriate, *Listen and write* the sentences from page 179.

Book Two

Book Two contains Chapters 1–6, Appendices A–F, and twelve stories.

Objectives of Book Two

Chapter 1: **Two-Syllable,** **Short-Vowel Words** **and Names**	Presents:

- two-syllable words using previously learned short vowels
- two-syllable words formed with the prefixes *un, ex, mis, dis, im, in*
- two-syllable words formed with the suffixes *ful, less, ness, es* (plural)
- sight words *for, or, want, too, women*
- multisyllabic words

Chapter 2: **Nouns and Verbs with Final s** **and Time-Related Words**	Presents:

- nouns and verbs
- past tense of *to be (was, were)*
- time-related words associated with *to be* and other verbs *(today, yesterday)*
- three uses of final **s:**

  1. third-person singular verb *(runs)*
  2. possessive *(Karen's)*
  3. plural *(seven dogs)*

Chapter 3: **Special Sounds**	Presents groups of related special sounds:

- **ck** *(lock),* **sh** *(ship),* **ch** *(check),* **tch** *(match)*
- **th** *(the, bath),* **wh** *(whip)*
- **ce** *(cent),* **ci** *(pencil),* **ge** *(gem),* **gi** *(rigid),* **dge** *(badge)*

Chapter 4: **Initial and Final Blends and** **Special Endings**	Presents initial blends with:

- **l** *(flag),* **r** *(crop)*
- **sc** *(scab),* **sk** *(sketch),* **sm** *(smell),* **sn** *(snip),* **sp** *(spell),* **st** *(step),* **sw** *(swam),* **tw** *(twin)*

Presents final blends with:

- **ct** *(act),* **ft** *(left)* **ld** *(held),* **lf** *(self),* **lk** *(milk),* **lm** *(elm),* **lp** *(help),* **lt** *(belt),* **mp** *(camp),* **nd** *(sand),* **nt** *(ant),* **pt** *(kept),* **sk** *(ask),* **st** *(fast),* **sp** *(wisp)*

Chapter 5: **Other Word Endings**	Presents other related word endings:

- **le** *(bubble),* **al** *(dental),* **y** *(happy),* **ly** *(sadly)*
- **ing** *(ring),* **ang** *(bang),* **ong** *(song),* **ung** *(sung),* **eng** *(length)*
- **ink** *(wink),* **ank** *(bank),* **onk** *(honk),* **unk** *(dunk),* **enk** *(Jenkins)*
- **ed = id** *(landed),* **ed = d** *(filled),* **ed = t** *(jumped)*
- **er** = noun *(runner),* **er** = adjective *(bigger)*

Chapter 6: **Contractions and** **Special Sounds**	Presents contractions with *to be* (present tense *is, am*):

- it**'s,** that**'s,** *noun***'s,** he**'s,** she**'s,** I**'m**

Presents contractions with *not:*

- isn't, aren't, wasn't, weren't, hasn't, haven't, can't

Presents special sounds:

- **y** = *ĭ (gym);* **ive** = *ĭv (live);* **tion** = *shun (mention)*

Appendices	The **Appendices** summarize and present examples of information and skills learned throughout Book Two.
Appendix A: **Sight Words**	Reviews sight words from Book One including:

- *to be,* colors, numbers, calendar, clock, and others

Summarizes new sight words from Book Two including:

- *for, or, want, too, women, today, yesterday, was, were, thing, nothing, something, think, thank, what, England, father, question*
- words and names in which **o** sounds like *ŭ (son)*
- words and names with the special sound of **u** *(pull)*

Appendix B: **Alphabetized List of Introductory Two-Syllable, Short-Vowel Words and Names**	Summarizes (in alphabetical order, for easy retrieval) the more than one hundred two-syllable words taught in Chapter 1 (pages 4–13).
Appendix C: **Geography**	Presents the names of major geographical areas that contain short vowels:

- countries, oceans, great rivers, cities, and other places
- United States (U.S.): states, capital cities, other cities

Appendix D: **Idioms**

- Summarizes the idioms taught in Book Two
- Presents additional idioms using the phonetic elements taught in Book Two, including definitions and sample sentences

Appendix E: **Common Last Names**

Presents samples of common last names used in Book Two:

- with short vowels
- with **y** endings
- color sight words
- for every letter of the alphabet (except **X**)

Appendix F: **Summary of Sounds and Words in the Stories in Book Two**

Summarizes for each of the twelve stories:

- phonetic elements
- sight words
- words and names with three or more syllables

Stories

Book Two contains twelve stories. They illustrate the specific phonetic elements taught in the previous sections of the current chapter and include for review some phonetic elements from earlier chapters. The themes of the stories center on adult concerns (work, health, law, interpersonal relations, and recreation) within the limits of the vocabulary and the phonetic elements students have learned.

If students have mastered the pages preceding the stories, they will be able to read them with ease. In fact, they will be amazed at the high level of complexity and achievement they have reached, even early in the book. The stories provide a great reward for learning.

How to Use the Major Teaching Devices

Three major teaching devices (the *Read, Write,* and *Listen and Write* sections) appear throughout the book and are the foundation of the *Essentials of Reading and Writing English* program.

Read

How to Use the *Read* Section

The mechanism of the *Read* section is basically the same for *Sounds, Words, Sentences,* and *Stories.*

As emphasized in Book One, concentrate on the sound of the vowel. When reading an individual sound, say the sound the letter makes, not the name of the letter. For example, on page 40 of the student text:

for **ck** = **k,** say *kuh,* not **c** *(see)* or **k** *(kay),* the letter names.

Start by reading the target sound, then build the words on the sound.

Explain to students that they are going to read the sound *kuh.* Point to **ck** at the top of the page and tell them that **ck** sounds like *kuh,* and point to **k.** Then say it sounds like *kuh* in the word *lock.* (Point to the illustration of a lock at the top right corner of page 40.)

Have students read *kuh, kuh, kuh* . . . across the top *Read* line. Then have them write **ck** on the *Write* line. When they are ready, you dictate *kuh* and they write **ck** on the *Listen and write* line.

Consider using the following successful reading strategies:

1. *Teacher reads first.* Read some examples to students. Ask them to listen and repeat what you read. For example, say:

Listen to the (sounds/words/sentences) I read. Listen especially for the (new/vowel) sounds. Look at the (sounds/words/ sentences) while I read them. Then read after me.

Note

Advantage of the Listen and repeat method: At the beginning, students can match sounds with letters.

Possible disadvantage: Students may chant and chorus by rote what they have just heard rather than read it.

---

2. *Students read first.* You then repeat what they say, correcting their pronunciation. (Do individual student reading, which is preferable; have group reading if necessary.)

Use either or both of the following strategies:

a. Chain reading. Have students read around the room. Indicate the order you want to use, having each student read one sound, word, or sentence in turn.

b. Random order reading. If students' attention wanders, do not preassign order. Call on them in random order. Not knowing when they will be called on will encourage them to follow along as the reading progresses.

Write

How to Use the *Write* Section

The mechanism of the *Write* section is basically the same for *Sounds, Words, Sentences,* and *Stories.*

1. Have students write only after reading. Decide if they should write after each item or at the end of the *Read* section. (It is usually preferable to write immediately after each item, since this reinforces both the reading and the writing.)

> **Note**
> Throughout the lesson, make sure that students' pronunciation is correct (or at least being attempted). Also check to ensure that they understand that particular letters represent particular sounds.

2. Allow students to use either hand printing or script.

> **Note**
> Encourage the use of script, since it is the most common form of written communication, especially for adults. Do not, however, discourage printing if it enables the reading to progress more smoothly. You and the students can always return to any point in the text to practice writing a passage in script. The object of the *Write* section is dual—to reinforce the reading and to write.

3. Have students copy the words, not write them from memory. Encourage them to look at the printed letters in the text before they write. This technique helps reinforce the similarities and differences between book type, hand printing, and script. Students will write from memory in the *Listen and write* section.

4. Encourage students to say each sound quietly to themselves as they write it.

5. Walk among the group to provide assistance, immediate correction, reassurance, and support.

Listen and write

How to Use the *Listen and write* Section

The mechanism of the *Listen and write* section is basically the same for *Sounds, Words, Sentences,* and *Stories.*

Listen and write is a critical part of the lesson. It forces students to focus their attention. It also indicates to them and to you whether or not they know the sound, word, or sentence. Students may think they hear the difference between the sounds, but it is only in *Listen and write* that they will see what they do and do not understand.

Although this section can be used as a test, its main objective is to clarify students' concepts of the sound before they progress to the next step—a slightly more advanced level.

Listen and write can be rewarding for many students, but very difficult for others. It is not necessary to complete all the *Listen and write* lines. Sometimes doing just a few will make the point. Sometimes all are needed as a review before advancing. Use your discretion in using this teaching tool to evaluate your own students' progress. As you begin *Listen and write:*

1. Tell students to use a piece of paper to cover the part of the page you will be dictating.

2. Dictate any or all of the sounds, words, sentences, or parts of sentences in the *Read* line, either in the order given or in random order.

3. Mark the order of the items you use in your own book.

When students have finished, write the list on the board, or have volunteers do so. Correct and compliment their attempts. Indicate that you know how difficult this work is, but explain that it will improve students' vocabulary, spelling, and listening skills. Then repeat the exercise, if desired, with a few more items. Any unused space on the paper can be used by students to practice writing the words they missed.

You might find it helpful at first to dictate only two or three items, stop and correct them, then proceed with another two or three. Don't overwhelm students. Never introduce a feeling of failure.

How to Use the Major Text Sections

Like the other books in this series, *Essentials of Reading and Writing English* Book Two makes use of the *Read, Write,* and *Listen and write* approach to learning. (See pages 58–60 of this manual for details.) These activities occur within the context of a patterned presentation of material. The sections described below appear throughout the book and should be handled the same way each time they appear. Read the general strategies for using each section described here, then refer to the specific chapter discussions for additions and variations to these strategies.

Sound and Sentences

Each sound is presented on two pages: a *Sound* page and a *Sentences* page. The emphasis in each of these two-page lessons is on building up and reinforcing already mastered skills. For example, see pages 40-44 of the student text.

The *Sound* page presents the target sound alone and in words. The *Sentences* page presents additional words and sentences featuring the target sound. The sounds, words, and sentences follow the basic methodology of *Read, Write,* and *Listen and write* as described on pages 58–60 of this manual.

Sound

How to Use the *Sound* Page

As the first page of each sound, it presents:

1. Sound: *Read, Write, Listen and write*

2. Compare: Contrast the target sound to other related but different or similar sounds and spellings: *Read, Write, Listen and write*

3. Words: A list of twelve simple words to *Read, Write, Listen and write*

Sound

Complete the *Sound* page, beginning at the top of the page.

Compare

The object of the *Compare* section is to clarify a new sound by comparing it to sounds and spellings already learned that are similar to or different from the target sound.

For example, see **ck = k** on page 40 of the student text. Read the *Compare* line. All the sounds are the same: **ck, c, k** all sound like **k = kuh.** At any point, stop and ask:

Is this sound the same as the one before? (Yes, in this case.) After students have read and written the sounds, dictate the *Listen and write* to them from the *Compare* lines.

If the sounds are the same (as in the case of **ck, c, k**) on the *Compare* lines, follow these steps:

1. Write the three spellings on the board.

2. Say the sound for each as you point to it. (Keep a record in your book.)

3. Have students write the sound, too, even though they see it.

In other cases, contrast is used to teach the target sound. For example, see *ch = chuh* on page 44 of the student text. It is important to emphasize that *ch* is a sound by itself, not a blend of *c (kuh)* and *h (huh)*. When you read the *Compare* line, tell students to listen to the different sounds: *ch (ch), c (kuh),* and *h (huh)*.

Words
The second half of the *Sound* page presents twelve common, usually one-syllable, words and names containing the target sound (for example, page 40 of the student text presents *lock, back, pack, sack, neck, pick, sick, Dick, sock, rock, luck, duck*). Students *Read* each word, then *Write* it immediately in the space provided. Point out that **ck** appears only at the end of words.

Note
Boldfacing the target sound facilitates recognition within a word. Be sure that students understand why the featured sound is darker than the other letters.

Sentences

How to Use the *Sentences* Page
As the second page for each target sound, the *Sentences* page presents:

1. Additional words in a box

2. Sentences to *Read* (usually six) containing several words with the target sound

3. *Write* lines for the sentences

4. *Listen and write* lines

Additional words box
The *Additional words* in the box are arranged in the order that would be most helpful to students—usually grouped by the short vowels, but sometimes listed alphabetically, or by the number of syllables. Sight words are set apart in the box. Point out the order of the words so students will recognize word families and notice similarities of spelling.

Read the *Additional words* with the class. If you think it is appropriate and not overwhelming for your students, have them *Write* and/or *Listen and write* some or all of the words. For extra practice, you may want to suggest that they write (or print) the words at home.

Encourage students not to be afraid of the multisyllabic words in the box. Show them that the larger words are made up of smaller parts, some of which they can already read. Remind them that they had experience at the beginning of Book Two with multisyllabic words (with short vowels and no special sounds). Having mastered each step along the way, they can progress with confidence to the next.

For example, see page 41 in the student text.
Say:

This box presents Additional words that contain the new sound *ck (kuh)*. The words are arranged in groups, by the vowel sounds that you already know—*ă, ĕ, ĭ, ŏ, ŭ,* such as (point to each at the top of the box) **ack, eck, ick, ock, uck.** Let's read the **ack** words. Read down the columns: *hack, Jack, lack,* . . . . Now let's read the **eck** words: *beck, deck.* Let's read the **ick** words: *hick, kick, lick, Mick, Nick,* . . . .
Notice how common this *ck (kuh)* sound is. Listen to the way these words rhyme: *hack, Jack, lack* . . . . Look how easy it is to spell these words: only the first letter changes in some of them (hack, Jack, lack); or only the vowel changes (hack, hick); or only the first two letters change (hack, beck). Just listen to one of these words and you can spell it. Not all words in English are spelled the way they sound, but many are, and this is a good way to begin learning.

Have students read the multisyllabic words last. Point out that they can already read parts of the words. Say:

You can read *un* and *pack,* so you can read *unpack;* you can read *rack* and *et,* so you can read *racket;* you can read *back* and *pack,* so you can read *backpack,* etc.

Sentences

Have students take turns reading one sentence at a time. Repeat it to clarify pronunciation. Ask questions to be sure that students understand the meaning. Explain new vocabulary if necessary. When it is clear that the class understands the sentence, read it again, then have students read it as a group.

> **Note**
> Emphasize the target sound. As an optional activity, have students underline the key sound in the sentences. (For example, on page 41 of the student text, ask: *Which words have ck (kuh) in sentence number one?* (duck's neck) To correct, students can add up the number of words they have underlined. Ask: *How many words did you underline? Which ones?*

Have students *Write* the sentences (either following each sentence or after all the sentences have been read). For *Listen and write,* dictate whole sentences or parts of sentences, depending on the ability of your students.

Sight Words ## How to Use the *Sight Words* Pages

Some sight words appear in the *Additional words* boxes on the *Sentences* pages. However, the most important sight words are presented on pages by themselves.
Explain that sight words do not follow the phonetic rules and they must be

memorized. (Students are already familiar with memorizing sight words from Book One.)

Note

Throughout Book Two, review the sight words from Book One, which are found in Appendix A.

Some of the sight words in Book Two will become *sound words* when students learn more phonetic rules as they progress in this text and continue to Book Three. However, others will always be sight words. Students should learn them now because they are common and useful words.

To teach the *sight words,* follow the *Read, Write,* and *Listen and write* strategies explained in "How to Use the Major Teaching Devices" on pages 58–60 of this manual. For example, page 13 of the student text presents four new sight words for students to memorize: *for, or, want,* and *too*. Explain that:

- *for* and *or* rhyme

- *too* sounds like *to* and *two* (which they know)

- *want* has a special sound of **a,** not like *apple.*

Review Pages

How to Use the *Review* Pages

Review pages appear periodically in the chapters and at the end of chapters, before the stories. (Pages 48 through 50 provide an example.) These reviews bring together all the phonetic elements taught in that section of the chapter. They also summarize the similarities and differences between the various sounds in the chapter section. Sentences that use words with the phonetic elements and sight words show students how the words sound in context and how to use them. They also provide an opportunity to compare and contrast the words.

Review pages consist of one or more pages of lists of words arranged in meaningful compare and contrast groups, if applicable, with a *Write* section, followed by a page of sentences that use the variety of sounds and words brought together in the previous review lists. The page ends with *Write* lines and a *Listen and write* section. Emphasize to your students the importance of listening carefully to the different sounds that you dictate.

Read sounds and words: (For example, see page 48.) Read across the page, from left to right. Compare sounds: **ch = *tch;*** point out that **ch** sounds harder than **sh; ck = k.**

Read sentences: (For example, see page 50.) Read each sentence. Have students look for different sounds in each sentence and underline the sounds that you specify. For example: sentence 1, *ck (wick), tch (match);* sentence 2, *sh (rush, shut, ship), tch (hatch);* sentence 3, *sh (codfish, shell);* sentence 4, *ch* and *ck (Chuck, check), sh (cash).*

Write: When students are ready to write the sentences, encourage them to say each one quietly to themselves before they write.

Listen and write: Before you dictate the sentences, tell students to cover the top part of the page. You can use either a fixed order or mixed order. Using mixed order is a valuable way to see if students are comprehending the material, not just memorizing it.

Additional Activities

These pages can be used in many different ways (underlining specific elements, creating new sentences, testing skills, etc.).

Bonus Pages

How to Use the *Bonus* Pages

The *Bonus* pages have different forms, but basically the same objective: to provide optional, challenging material for advanced or enthusiastic students. Using the *Bonus* pages is not required, but can be challenging and fun if students have mastered previous work. These pages present new material alone and in sentences. (For example, see student text pages 18 and 19.)

Bonus Page Words
(for example, see page 18)

Explain that three- and four-syllable words are like two-syllable ones, except that they have more parts, forming a chain of syllables. Point out that the students already know the parts; for example, the word *inhabit* in sentence 4. Two of the syllables, *in* and *it,* are known words; the other, *hab,* has a known sound, *ă.* Present these multisyllabic words in the same way that you presented the two-syllable words on text pages 4 through 7.

Bonus Page sentences
(for example, see page 19)

Read the sentences, then have students write them. Dictate the *Listen and write* after the other reading and writing has been completed. (Follow the general *Read, Write,* and *Listen and write* guidelines on pages 58–60 of this manual.)

Note
Bonus pages are found in the following chapters in the student text: Chapter 1, pages 18–19; Chapter 4, pages 114–117; Chapter 6, page 215.

Stories

How to Use the *Stories*

Objectives

- To use the phonetic elements and sight words learned so far in a meaningful context

- To give students a sense of accomplishment

Emphasize to students that they can read these stories because they have already learned the phonetic elements from which they are built. The stories will provide positive reinforcement to students.

Phonetic Specifications

Each story is followed by a chart of sounds, sight words, and multisyllabic words that are emphasized in the story. The chart also lists sounds and words from previous stories. Tell students that the current story has sounds that they already know; if you think it will be helpful, read the lists of sounds and sight words with them. (Appendix F provides a summary of the sounds and sight words used in the stories.)

Themes

The stories expose students to a wide scope of topics and technical information. The main characters, drawn from a cross-section of the ethnic richness in the United States, serve as role models with which students can identify.

The stories in Book Two cover the following themes:

Story 1: The Picnic at Cactus Canyon (page 16)
  Theme: Family and friends picnic at a park in the southwest United States. Relationships, games, and food are highlighted.

Story 2: Helen's Lesson (page 37)
> *Theme:* A young woman, working and studying part-time, is failing in school and having interpersonal problems on the job. After some soul-searching, she changes her attitude and behavior and finds success.

Story 3: Chen's Chuck Wagon (page 51)
> *Theme:* A hard-working young man runs a mobile lunchwagon with the help of an equally hard-working young woman friend.

Story 4: Justice Comes to Ridgeton (page 69)
> *Theme:* Court convenes in a small town. Members of the community pack the courthouse as diverse cases come before the judge and the jury with various resolutions.

Story 5: The Drop-In Clinic (page 89)
> *Theme:* Many services are offered in this neighborhood health clinic. Some of the specialties and the doctors who provide them are described.

Story 6: Camp West Wind (page 102)
> *Theme:* A multitude of activities are available at this family camp in Florida. There is recreation for adults and children, including a drama workshop. At the end, the camp's benefactors are acknowledged.

Story 7: Trent's Dress and Pants Shop (page 110)
> *Theme:* A wide variety of quality clothing is displayed and sold at the manufacturer's on-site retail store. Then the "inner workings" of a clothing store are described: working conditions, people's skills and specialties, and teamwork.

Story 8: The Dance Academy's Festival (page 133)
> *Theme:* The principal of a dance academy successfully organizes and runs a potluck supper and dance festival.

Story 9: The Franklin Fish Packing Plant (page 164)
> *Theme:* Many of the steps involved in processing and packing fish in a large factory are described. Workers' attitudes toward their jobs and supportive relationships among coworkers are also noted.

Story 10: We Visited Uncle Ned's Cattle Ranch (page 183)
> *Theme:* A suburban family visits the midwestern cattle ranch of an uncle. How they deal with packing up and closing their home is described, as well as their participation in ranch activities.

Story 11: Mr. Webster's Day at the Bunker Hill Bank (page 202)
> *Theme:* Many of the services provided by a major bank in New England are described. The bank manager, a "proper Bostonian," his customers, and the services they require are introduced. The story also describes the romance developing between Mr. Webster and Beverly Anderson, a trust officer of the bank.

Story 12: The Crystal Junction Banner (page 226)
> *Theme:* A newspaper-style article describes a speech given by a member of Congress at a political rally. Citizens' reactions to this presidential candidate are also reported.

Vocabulary

The vocabulary taught in the stories emphasizes the phonetic content of the lessons (as noted previously and in Appendix F). Within the limits of the phonetic elements, the vocabulary offers students growing expertise and awareness of the terminology in these areas:

Story 1: food; recreation; relationships among family members and pets

Story 2: attitude and behavior at school and on the job

Story 3: food preparation; self-employment; factory products

Story 4: law; legal decision-making; crime and punishment

Story 5: personal health; medical care and options

Story 6: nature; camp activities—swimming, boating, land sports, dramatics

Story 7: varieties of clothing and fabrics; manufacturing process and types of skills needed; modeling; selling; alterations; interpersonal work attitudes

Story 8: organization and planning skills; party decorations; cooperation; food for a potluck supper; different kinds of dances; music; city transportation

Story 9: fish packing and processing; general factory procedures; working closely and cooperatively with others

Story 10: suburban and farm life; suburban home maintenance, repairs, and responsibilities; ranch flora and fauna; ranch hands' chores and recreation; extended family relationships

Story 11: banking and finance problems and options; one type of courtship

Story 12: newspaper style and reporting; politics and campaigning; voter response to a candidate

Previewing Key Words

As the stories advance in Book Two, they contain more multisyllabic words, which are introduced in the pages preceding each story (entitled "Previewing Words of Three or More Syllables from . . ."). The words are presented alphabetically, both as whole words and divided into syllables. (Standard for syllabification and definitions: *Webster's Ninth New Collegiate Dictionary,* Merriam-Webster, 1986.) When there is a disparity between the number of syllables in the common pronunciation and the dictionary syllabification, the pronunciation is presented.

Read the example words in syllables for students and have them repeat. Then read the whole word, with students chorusing. For example, see page 68. Read **a—gen—da; agenda.** Have individuals continue reading the list, one word (in syllables and whole) at a time, as you repeat to clarify pronunciation, and the class repeats in chorus. Encourage the class to look at the words and read them as they chorus, not just repeat them by ear, which is the temptation. (But even if students repeat by ear, such repetition is better than nothing, since it reinforces pronunciation. The chain reading guarantees each student a chance to read aloud.)

For *Listen and write,* dictate whole words only.

After students have read the *Previewing* pages, they will be prepared to read everything in the stories. These multisyllabic words have the specific sounds taught in this and previous chapters, and they contain nothing that students have not already learned. If the readability level appears high, it is still quite masterable and can be used to students' advantage. As long as the words are presented in the context of merely linking sounds and syllables already learned, students will not be overwhelmed.

Instructional Sequence for the *Stories*

1. *Read aloud in class:* Students may prepare ahead of class by reading silently or aloud to themselves at home, but this is not required. Read around the room, chain reading. Indicate the order you want to use, having each student read one sentence. If students' attention wanders, call on them in random order. Not knowing when they will be called on will encourage them to follow along as the reading progresses.

2. *Call attention to the subheadings:* Explain that each subhead tells the theme of the paragraph(s) that follows. Encourage students to use subheads as clues to the subject. (For example, see student text page 110, subheads **The Catalog, Fabrics.**)

3. *Ask questions to ensure comprehension:* Discussion questions for each story are suggested in this Teacher's Manual. The questions are numbered to correspond to the paragraphs in the story, so that you can help students find the answers easily. In addition, try to relate the stories to the lives of your students by asking such questions as *Have you ever done this? Do you know anyone who has? How did you feel? What would you recommend?*

> **Note**
> The stories are adult-oriented and contain valuable work-related vocabulary. They become progressively more complex phonetically, but even at a simple level in the early stories, there is a surprisingly large amount of technical vocabulary presented. Be sure to point out how much students can already read, even at their present level.

4. *Optional skill reinforcement:* Have students underline words in the story that include specific sounds with which you think they need help. They may do this underlining before or after they read. Sometimes it is helpful to have them do this before the reading to reinforce the idea that they know the sounds in these passages (if they seem overwhelmed). But do not make it tedious; sometimes underlining one paragraph is enough. Overall, reading the stories should be fun, not complicated with burdensome extra tasks.

5. *Optional class activities:*

   a. Use the stories (particularly *Story 4: Justice Comes to Ridgeton*) as plays. Have students take roles and act out the parts. They can read from the text, memorize the dialogue, or invent their own lines.

   b. Artistically inclined students may want to draw their interpretations of a particular story.

6. *Optional field trips:* Visit places like the ones identified in the stories—parks, colleges, stores, hospitals, banks, political candidates' offices, and newspapers. Some of these might offer free literature for students to read. Visit the local library for literature, calendar of events, and to get an idea of services offered; some students may want to sign up for library cards.

   Possible field trips for each story include the following: *Story 1:* public park, conservation land, botanical garden; *Story 2:* office building or small restaurant, community college; *Story 3:* fish pier or market, mobile lunchwagon, factory outlet; *Story 4:* courthouse (with trial in session, if possible); *Story 5:* health center, clinic, or hospital; *Story 6:* camp in the country, local drama groups; *Story 7:* clothing factory and/or store; *Story 8:* school- or community-sponsored dance (serving refreshments or potluck supper); *Story 9:* fish packing plant; *Story 10:* ranch or farm; *Story 11:* bank; *Story 12:* town meeting or town hall, political rally or campaign headquarters, local newspaper.

Chapter 1: Two-Syllable, Short-Vowel Words and Names

Complete this chapter following the suggestions in "How to Use the Major Teaching Devices" and "How to Use the Major Text Sections" on pages 58–67 of this manual. Variations are noted below.

Page 2 ## Introduction to Two-Syllable, Short-Vowel Words

Review the basic concepts of short vowels and one-syllable words taught in Book One.

Page 3 ## Two-Syllable, Short-Vowel Words

Write the word *sunset* on the board. Read it (and explain the meaning if necessary). Underline the **u** in *sun* as you say it, then the **e** in *set*. Lead students through the six steps. Wait for them to respond.

Pages 4–8 ## 100 Two-Syllable, Short-Vowel Words

Tell students that this lesson offers a hundred two-syllable words—long words—that they can read, using what they have already learned. Use *sunset* as an example. Say:

Repeat after me: *sun set, sunset; hub cap, hubcap.*

Praise students. Continue in this fashion or read in unison with the class. You can also have students take turns reading around the room, or you can have one student read a word, then you repeat it, followed by the class echoing it. For example:

Student: nap kin, napkin

Teacher: *(correcting if necessary)* nap kin, napkin

Class: nap kin, napkin

At the bottom of page 7, point out the three sight words *(women, bullet, welcome)*.

Pages 9–10 ## Two-Syllable, Short-Vowel Words Formed with Prefixes and Suffixes

Page 9 ### Prefixes *un, ex, mis, dis, im, in*

Explain that prefixes are special kinds of syllables in two-syllable words. Point out that they affect the meaning of the word, but that words with prefixes are pronounced like other two-syllable words.

Have students write all of the prefixes before they do the *Listen and write*. If you want, dictate the words in random order. (They don't have to match the words printed on the lines.)

Page 10 ### Suffixes *ful, less, ness, es* (plural)

Explain that a suffix comes at the end of a word. Point out that words with suffixes are handled like other two-syllable words.

Have students write all of the suffixes before they do the *Listen and write*. If you want, dictate the words in random order. (They don't have to match the words printed on the lines.)

| **Page 11** | ## Two-Syllable, Short-Vowel Words and Names in which o Sounds Like ŭ *(sun)* |

Page 11

Two-Syllable, Short-Vowel Words and Names in which o Sounds Like ŭ *(sun)*

Call attention to these two-syllable words whose endings rhyme with *sun, some, come* (sight words in Book One).

Page 12

Two-Syllable, Short-Vowel Names

Explain that these are names of people. Point out that women's names and men's names are in separate lists. Explain the footnotes.

Page 13

Sight Words *for, or, want, too*

See "How to Use the *Sight Words* Pages" on pages 62–63 of this manual.

Pages 14–15

Sentences with Two-Syllable, Short-Vowel Words

Follow these steps:

1. Have students take turns reading aloud.

2. Repeat what each student has just read, correcting pronunciation when necessary.

3. Have the class repeat in chorus.

You may want the class to read all of the sentences, then write them, or to alternate reading and writing. You may prefer to have students write the sentences for homework.
Listen and write after *Write*. Dictate either complete sentences or phrases.

> **Note**
> Corrections made on the spot are most effective; don't wait until the lesson is over.

Pages 16–17

Story 1: The Picnic at Cactus Canyon

The skills consolidated in this story cover Chapter 1. (See "How to Use the *Stories*" on pages 64–67 of this manual.)

> **Note**
> Phonetic specifications are listed after the story.

Additional Activities

Have students underline the two-syllable, short-vowel words and names.

Discussion Questions

Select from the following questions those that are appropriate for your class; ask other questions. Encourage students to respond, to give their answers and opinions, and to ask additional questions. This will help them comprehend the information in the story and gain confidence in their growing abilities.

Paragraph 1: What is a picnic? Where in the United States is this picnic taking place? *(in the southwest)* What is a cactus? *(a desert plant that needs little water and grows in a hot, dry climate; it usually has spines on its fleshy stem; some have flowers)* What is a canyon? *(a deep valley, often with water streaming through it)* (NOTE: If possible, display a map of the United States and point to Texas, New Mexico, Arizona, Southern California, and Nevada. Tell students that the picnic may have taken place in any of these states, because a variety of cacti flourish there. You might want to show pictures of cacti to the class.)

Paragraph 2: Who is at this picnic?

Paragraph 3: What are the picnickers eating?

Paragraph 4: What "wild" animals come up to the kids? (If appropriate, ask students to describe a rabbit, a robin, an ant, a bug.)

Paragraph 5: What pets did the kids bring with them? (If appropriate, ask students the difference between pets and wild animals. Call attention to the number of animals mentioned in Paragraphs 4 and 5: two rabbits, seven robins, one cat, seven kittens, two dogs.)

Paragraphs 6–7: What activity are the adults doing?

Paragraph 8: What is talent?

Paragraph 9: What is comic talent?

Paragraph 10: What activities are the kids doing? How many kids are there? (NOTE: If possible, display a compass or a picture of one and ask: What is a compass? *a small instrument that shows direction; it has a needle that points to magnetic north)*

Paragraph 11: Was the picnic fun? Do the picnickers want to come again?

Additional questions: Have you ever been on a picnic? Where did you go? What did you eat? What did you do?

Page 18   **Bonus Page: Short-Vowel Words with Three or More Syllables**

See "How to Use the *Bonus* Pages" on page 64 of this manual.

Page 19   **Bonus Page: Sentences Using Short-Vowel Words with Three or More Syllables**

See "How to Use the *Bonus* Pages" on page 64 of this manual.

Chapter 2: Nouns and Verbs with Final *s* and Time-Related Words

Complete this chapter following the suggestions in "How to Use the Major Teaching Devices" and "How to Use the Major Text Sections" on pages 58–67 of this manual. Variations are noted below.

Page 22 ## Introduction to Nouns and Verbs

Introduce the concept of nouns, plural nouns, and verbs. You might want to tell students that verbs are "action words."

Answer key:

A. The nouns to be circled are: *cats, ants, dogs, kids.*

B. The verbs to be underlined are: *sit, dig, run, nap.*

C. The nouns to be circled are: *mitts, men, kids, rat, kin, bugs, bats, ax, van, Dads, Moms, cabs.* The verbs to be underlined are: *fit, sit, visit, nips, kiss, hop, sip, jabs, hits, gab, hug, ram.*

Page 23 ## Sight Words: *today, yesterday*

See "How to Use the *Sight Words* Pages" on pages 62–63 of this manual.

Introduce the sight words *today* and *yesterday.* Remind students that they know the word *day* (from days of the week: Book One, Life Skills). Point out that the *to* in *today* sounds like the sight word *to* that they learned in Book One, and that the *yes* in *yesterday* is a sound word they learned in Book One.

Page 24 ## Sentences Using *today, yesterday*

Compare *yesterday* (past) and *today* (present).

Page 25 ## Verb Tenses with *today, yesterday*

Read the chart of present and past tense of some common verbs (verbs with **ed** endings will be taught in Chapter 5). Help students fill in the blanks with the appropriate words.

Page 26 ## Sight Words: *was, were* (past tense of the verb *to be*)

This lesson expands the concept of the past tense of *to be.*

Call attention to the sight words, explaining that they do not follow the rules. Then read aloud, having students repeat after you.

Page 27 ## Sentences Using *was, were* (past tense of the verb *to be*)

Each item has two sentences, one using present tense, the other using past tense. You may want to remind students that the period at the end of each sentence indicates a complete idea.

To further illustrate the concept of time, have students invent other sets of sentences. These should be said aloud, not written. The emphasis at this point should be on contrasting present and past.

Page 28   ## Verb + s = Third-Person Singular

This lesson introduces the third-person singular. Write the example with *run* on the board, underlining the **s** in *he/she/it runs*. Be sure that students understand that the other examples of *run* don't need an **s**.

Pages 29–30   ## Verbs with and without s

Read across the page, left to right. Work with students to compare the columns. After reading the entire page, read down the right-hand column, emphasizing the rhythm of the repeated *he, she, it, he, she, it*.

   Listen and write: Dictate as many of the following as are appropriate for your class.

1. Verbs *(run, sit, get, runs, sits, gets)*

2. Pronoun and verb combinations *(I run, she runs, they win, he naps)*

3. Sentences using nouns from previous pages and Book One *(The dog runs. The dogs run. The cat naps. The cats nap. The kid sits. The kids sit.)*

Page 31   ## Sentences Using Verbs with and without s

Compare different verb endings. Note that the lesson gets progressively more difficult.

   The first section of the page compares the endings of the same verb in the two parts of the sentence: 1. I **get** a basket, and he **gets** a bag. The second section compares the endings of different verbs: 1. I **hem** the bottoms, and he **pins** the tops.

Page 32   ## Noun + 's = Possessive

A. Explain that for singular nouns, we add **'s** as follows: for a person by name: **Karen's;** for a person: **man's;** for an animal: **kitten's;** for an object: **cabin's;** when a singular noun ends in **s: cactus's.**

B. Explain that for plural nouns that end in **s,** we just add an apostrophe (**'**). Provide examples, such as: the **dogs'** tags; the **cats'** baskets. Ask volunteers to think of additional examples.

C. Explain that for plural nouns that do not end in **s,** we add **'s.** Provide examples, such as: the **men's** cabs; the **mice's** hole.
   This is an especially important lesson for students to *Listen and write.*

Page 33   ## Sentences with 's

Read around the room, then have students write the sentences. Dictate the *Listen and write* in fixed or mixed order.

Pages 34–36   ## Review: Final s

A. Nouns—Singular and Plural

Remind students that **s** at the end of a word can have three meanings. Read across the top of the page, pointing out that the first column shows the examples in singular form.

Answer key:

1. one melon	5. five napkins	9. eight wagons
2. two hubcaps	6. a camel	10. nine salads
3. three lemons	7. six hens	11. ten muffins
4. four cabins	8. seven bandits	12. an attic

> **Note**
> Be sure that students understand that *a* and *an* = *one*.

B. Nouns—Possessive

Answer key:

1. the dog's leg	5. Janet's doll	9. the kid's tonsils
2. the basket's ribbon	6. the caftan's button	10. a cactus's pot
3. the pens' tips	7. Adam's lesson	11. Mrs. Wilson's job
4. a man's hat	8. a hen's egg	12. Dennis's exam

C. Verbs

Answer key:

1. I visit	5. it happens	8. they sell
2. you quit	6. we upset	9. you and I exit
3. he jogs	7. you win	10. he and she sublet
4. she cuts		

D. Nouns and Verbs—Singular and Plural

Answer key:

1. hops	4. run	7. tug
2. rabbits	5. pulls	8. cat
3. dog	6. camels	9. tugs

Pages 37–38   ## Story 2: Helen's Lesson

This story consolidates the skills taught in Chapter 2. (See "How to Use the *Stories*" on pages 64–67 of this manual.)

> **Note**
> Phonetic specifications are listed after the story.

Additional Activities

After students have read the story, have them underline verb + **s** (third-person singular); circle noun + **'s** (possessive); and box noun + **s** (plural).

Discussion Questions

Select from the following questions those that are appropriate for your class; ask other questions. Encourage students to respond, to give their answers and opinions, and to ask additional questions. This will help them comprehend the information in the story and gain confidence in their growing abilities.

Note

Explain the following concepts in the story:

Idioms (see Appendix D): *sass me; tell me off* = to act in a disrespectful manner (unprofessional and unacceptable at work); *let go* = fired from a job

Words that sound alike but have different spellings and meanings: *lesson* = something to be learned; *lessen* = to make or become less

---

Paragraph 1: Does Helen have a job today? *(no)* Did she have one yesterday? *(yes)* Was Helen "let go"? What does "let go" mean? *(fired)* Who fired Helen? *(Mrs. Wilson)* Who is Mrs. Wilson? *(Helen's boss)* Why was Helen fired? *(She behaved badly at work.)* Was Helen doing well at school? *(No; she didn't pass her exams.)*

Paragraph 2: Does Mrs. Wilson think there is hope for Helen? *(yes)* Why? *(Helen "has a lot of talent.")* Does Mrs. Wilson suggest ways for Helen to improve? *(Yes: "go to the campus"; "get on with the lessons"; "get some input")* (NOTE: Explain that *getting input* means to get ideas and advice from others. *Input* comes from computer terminology and means coded information fed into a computer system.)

Paragraph 3: Can Helen afford to keep her apartment? *(no)* Who does she ask to live with? *(Mom and Dad)* Do they take her in? *(yes)* (NOTE: If appropriate for your students, ask what they think about grown children who are in trouble going home to live with a parent or parents). Are they happy or upset with Helen? *(upset)* When she discusses her problems with them, what do Mom and Dad suggest? *(She should do well with her lessons.)*

Paragraph 4: Where is Helen's exam? Is it a big exam or a little quiz?

Paragraph 5: How does Helen feel about taking the exam? *(She is upset; she panics; she wants to vomit.)* Is Helen strong and determined now? *(Yes; she says "I have to pass or I will not have a job!")*

Note

Ask students what the exclamation mark means. If necessary, remind them that they learned in Book One that it shows strong feelings.

Call attention to *lesson* and *lessen*. "I have had a lesson" means that I have learned something; "Her panic lessens" means that her panic grows smaller.

Discuss with students what *lesson* means in the larger sense. In Helen's case, her poor attitude and misbehavior led to her failing her courses and losing her job. When she says, "I have had a lesson," she has learned that it is her responsibility and within her control to study so that she can succeed, and to act in a professional, respectful manner toward other people at work. She has learned about cause and effect: if you don't study, you will probably fail; if you are rude and disrespectful, you will probably get fired.

Paragraph 6: What does Mrs. Wilson do when Helen visits her after the exam? *(She gives Helen a job, encourages her to continue her education, discusses her potential: "You have talent with no limit and you will do well.")*

Chapter 3: Special Sounds

Complete this chapter following the suggestions in "How to Use the Major Teaching Devices" and "How to Use the Major Text Sections" on pages 58–67 of this manual. Variations are noted below.

Chapter 3 teaches twelve new sounds:

- *ck, sh, ch,* and *tch* are taught first. These lessons are followed by *Story 3: Chen's Chuck Wagon,* which emphasizes these sounds.

- *th* (with and without throat), *wh, ce, ci, ge, gi,* and *dge* are presented next. These lessons are followed by *Story 4: Justice Comes to Ridgeton,* which emphasizes these sounds.

Pages 40-41   ck = *k* Sound and Sentences

Page 40   Tell students that **ck** appears only at the end of a word.

Page 41   *Haddock* is a sight word (see Appendix A).

Pages 42-43   *sh* Sound and Sentences

Page 42   *Compare: shuh, suh, huh.* Explain that **sh** makes one new sound *(shuh)*, not *suhhuh.* Point out that **sh** can come at the beginning or at the end of a word or syllable, as in *ship* and *cash.* Be sure students see that items 1 through 7 have **sh** at the beginning and that items 8 through 12 have **sh** at the end.

Page 43   *Additional words box:* Explain that sometimes the sound appears twice in the same words, as in *shellfish* and *shellshock.* Ask:

Do you see **ck** from the last lesson? *(shack, shellshock, shock, shuck)*

> **Note**
> *Push* and *bush* are sight words; **u** has the sound of *pull* and *bull.*

Pages 44–45   *ch* Sound and Sentences

Page 44   *Compare: chuh, kuh, huh.* Explain that **ch** makes one new sound *(chuh),* not *kuhhuh.* Tell students that **ch** can appear at the beginning and at the end of a word or syllable.

> **Note**
> *About sexist language:* In Chapters 3 and 4, a few two-syllable words that end in *man* are introduced, for example, *henchman, freshman.* You may want to ask students if they understand that English words ending in *man* refer to both men and women. Explain that they will sometimes see and hear words such as *fireman, policeman, draftsman, sportsmanship, fisherman.* Encourage students to use more appropriate alternatives, such as *police officer, fire fighter, drafter, crew member.* For more detailed information, see *The Handbook of Nonsexist Writing* by Casey Miller and Kate Swift, Harper & Row, 1980 and *The Nonsexist Word Finder* by Rosalie Maggio, Oryx Press, 1987. These excellent references offer useful suggestions on how to avoid sexist language and provide workable alternatives to words ending in *man.*

Pages 46–47   *tch* Sound and Sentences

Page 46   *Compare:* Explain that **tch** sounds like *ch.* Tell students that **tch** appears only at the end of a word or syllable.

<table>
<tr><td>**Pages 48–49**</td><td># Review: Words with ck, ch, tch, sh</td></tr>
</table>

Pages 48–49

Review: Words with ck, ch, tch, sh

Page 48   Emphasize similarities (**ch** = *tch*) and differences (**ch** harder than **sh**; **ck** different). Point out that words are usually the same except for the part changed by the special sound *(chip/ship; much/muck)*.

Page 49   Dictate the *Listen and write* in any order. Select examples of comparisons from page 48 and from pages 40–47.

Page 50

Review: Sentences with ck, ch, tch, sh

Additional Activities
Have students underline **ch, tch**; circle **sh**; box **ck.**

Pages 51–52

Story 3: Chen's Chuck Wagon
This story consolidates the sounds and skills learned in the first part of Chapter 3 *(ck, ch, tch, sh)*. It also includes selections from previous lessons and from Book One to reinforce learning.

Note
Phonetic specifications are listed after the story. If appropriate for your students, you might want to read this information to them.

Additional Activities
Have students mark (underline, circle, box, highlight) the new sounds *ch, tch, sh,* and *ck.*

Discussion Questions
Select from the following questions those that are appropriate for your class; ask other questions. Encourage students to respond, to give their answers and opinions, and to ask additional questions. This will help them comprehend the information in the story and gain confidence in their growing abilities.

Paragraph 1: What is a hatchback? *(a car with a compartment in the back with an upward-opening door [hatch])* What is a chuck wagon? *(In this story, a chuck wagon is a portable kitchen. In the Old West, it was the wagon that carried the cook, the food [chuck], and the cooking equipment. This was mostly done for cowboys who were herding cattle or sheep out on the range, away from the ranch house.)* What does Chen use his hatchback for? *(to sell lunch)*

Paragraph 2: Who is Hanna? *(Chen's chum)* What is her job? *(to go to the docks and get fish; to work with Chen)* Does Hanna encourage Chen when he gets worried about money? *(yes)*

Paragraph 3: What does Hanna tell Chen? *(Do not be upset. You will get lots of cash when the fish is sold for lunch.)*

Paragraph 5: Where do Chen and Hanna clean and cook the fish? *(in a rustic shed on the dock)* (Explain: *rustic* = rough, unfinished.)

Paragraphs 5 and 6: What do they do to the fish? *(They shuck the shellfish; cut and chop the fish; put fish in the oven until it is hot and brown.)* What kind of fish do they work on? *(catfish, shad, bass, codfish)* Where will they sell the lunch? *(at Mitchell's Jacket Shop)*

Paragraph 7: What do the people who work at Mitchell's Jacket Shop do? *(cut, hem and tack jackets; put patch pockets on jackets; match socks and sashes to jackets; do shag rugs and mesh bags)*

Paragraph 8: At what time do Hanna and Chen arrive at Mitchell's? *(11:45 A.M.)* Is this time close to noon? *(yes)* How many minutes to noon? *(15 minutes)*

Paragraph 9: Do Chen and Hanna sell a lot of food at Mitchell's? *(yes)* (NOTE: Explain: *itch for* = to want something a lot. In this case, people want lunch.) Do all the workers at Mitchell's buy lunch at the Chuck Wagon? *(No; some bring their food in a lunch box.)*

Paragraphs 10 and 11: Does Chen's Chuck Wagon sell everything people ask for? *(no)* What didn't Chen have? *(hash, chicken, chitlins, hot dogs)* (Explain: hash is made of small pieces of leftover cooked meat mixed with vegetables and gravy; chitlins [also spelled chitterlings and chitlings] are the small intestines of a pig, cooked for food.)

Paragraphs 12 and 13: (If necessary, explain that punch is usually made from fruit juices and is served chilled.)

Paragraph 14: Do Chen and Hanna clean up after the lunch hour? *(yes)* What do they do? *(They pick up the mess, pack it up, toss it into a bucket; put the bucket in the hatchback, lock up Chen's Chuck Wagon.)*

Paragraph 15: Did lunch at the Chuck Wagon bring in a lot of cash? *(yes)*

Paragraph 16: Did Hanna get paid? *(yes)* Was Chen happy? *(yes)*

General Questions

1. Do you know anyone who has a mobile (moving) lunch wagon like Chen's? (If it is the case in your region of the country, you may want to point out that these vehicles are called "canteens." They often drive around to large manufacturing companies and factories.) Is it a hatchback or another style car or truck?

2. Does anyone in the class work in a factory like Mitchell's Jacket Shop?

3. Do you bring your lunch or do you buy it? Where? Is it expensive? Is it cheap?

Pages 53–54

th (with throat) Sound and Sentences

Emphasize that this *th* sound comes from the throat. Demonstrate by putting your hand to your larynx to feel the vibration. Encourage students to do the same.

Page 53   *Compare:* Ensure that students understand that ***thuh*** is different from ***tuh*** and ***huh***.

Page 54   There are no additional words for the *th* (with throat) sound at this point in the learning process.

Pages 55–56

th (no throat) Sound and Sentences

Emphasize that with this *th* sound, students should feel no vibration in the throat. Have them put their hands on the larynx and practice the sound, using tongue and teeth only.

Page 55   *Compare:* *the* (vibration) and *bath* (no vibration). Sounds like ***thuh*** (no throat) and different from ***tuh*** and ***huh***.

Words: Explain that **th** (no throat) can come at the beginning and at the end of a word.

> **Note**
> Point out the sight words (items 9 through 12) *thing, nothing, think, thank.* Tell students that these words follow rules that they will learn in Chapter 5.

Page 56

Additional Activities
Have students underline the words with **th** (no throat) and circle those with **th** (with throat).

Explain that in the word *month,* **o** = *ŭ* (as in *sun*).

Pages 57–58

wh (feel your breath) Sound and Sentences
Demonstrate how to achieve this sound. Ask students to hold one hand in front of the mouth, purse the lips, breathe out, and say **wh**. Tell them they should feel the air as they make the sound.

Page 57

Compare: white (feel air); *wig* (feel no air); *huh* (feel little air)

> **Note**
> Point out the sight words *what* and *white*. Compare the sounds in *what* and *hat*; compare *white* with *wit, hit,* and *whit.* Explain that *what* and *white* have sounds that will be taught in Book Three.

Page 58

Additional Activities
Have students underline words with **wh**, circle those with **w**.

Page 59

Sound c = *s* (before e and i)
Remind students that until now, they have used the hard sound **kuh** for the letter **c**. Say and write on the board *cat, cot, cut.* Explain that the letter **c** usually sounds hard before the vowels **a, o,** and **u.** Point out those vowels in the words on the board.

Now tell students that they are going to learn a new sound (the soft sound **suh**) for the letter **c**. Point to the words at the top of the page, and say *cent* and *pencil.*

Compare: **ce** = *se;* **ci** = *si;* ca = *ka;* **co** = *ko;* **cu** = *ku.* Make sure students are saying the correct sound.

The top line reads *se, se, si, si, se, si, se, si, se, si, se, si.*

The bottom line reads *ka, ko, ku, se, si, ka, se, si, ko, ku, se, si.*

Page 60

Comparing and Contrasting Words with ce, ci, ca, co, cu
Go over steps 1 through 3 with students. Work with them to compare and contrast the sounds and words with **ce, ci.** Be sure they understand that **ce, ci** have the soft sound of *se, si.* Then go over steps 4 through 6. Compare and contrast the sound and words with **ca, co,** and **cu,** pointing out that these have the hard sound of *kuh.* (*Cecil* is the word that has both soft sounds of **ce** and **ci** in it.)

Be sure that students see that the two charts are different. The top chart has words with the soft sounds of **ce, ci.** The bottom chart has words with the hard sounds of **ca, co,** and **cu.** Have students read down the columns. (*Cancel* is the word with both the hard sound of **ca** and the soft sound of **ce.**)

Page 61 ## Sentences: Comparing and Contrasting Words with Hard and Soft c

Use the two charts on page 60 as the additional word boxes for this lesson.

Additional Activities

Have students underline the soft **ce** and **ci** in words and circle the hard **ca, co,** and **cu** in words.

Page 62 ## Sound: g = *j* before e and i (soft)

Remind students that until now they have been using the hard sound **guh** for the letter **g**. Say and write on the board *gas, got, gut.* Explain that the letter **g** usually sounds hard before the vowels **a, o,** and **u**. Point out those vowels in the words on the board. Add that **g** acts just like the soft **c** that they learned about in the last lesson.

Now tell students that they are going to learn a new sound (the soft sound **juh**) for the letter **g**. Point to the words at the top of the page and say *gem* and *rigid.* Explain that the letter **g** sounds like **j** before the vowels **e** and **i**. Then read the line of **ge** (*je*), **gi** (*ji*).

Compare: **ge** = *je,* **gi** = *ji,* **ga** = *ga,* **go** = *go,* **gu** = *gu.* Make sure students are saying the correct sound.

The top line reads *je, je, ji, ji, ga, go, gu, je, ji, ga, go, gu.*
The bottom line reads *je, ji, je, ji, je, ji, je, ji, je, ji, ga, je.*

Page 63 ## Sentences Using Words with the *ge, gi* Sounds

Call attention to the three separate boxes of words. The first one has two additional words with **ge, gi;** the second contains words where **ge, gi** make a hard sound. Point out that these are special cases. The third box offers a review of the letter **g** with the hard sound in **ga, go, gu.** Remind students that they already know the one-syllable words in the second and third boxes (*gimmick* and *given* are new).

Review the words with **ga, go, gu,** making the hard sound. Contrast them with some soft-sound words.

Additional Activities

Have students underline the words with the soft sound of **ge, gi** only. Omit the rest; they may be too confusing for students at this point.

Pages 64–65 ## dge = *ge, je* Sound and Sentences

Explain that **dge** sounds the same as **ge, je.** Tell students to ignore the **d** when they say words with **dge.**

Page 64 *Compare:* Remind students that all the sounds are like *je.*

Page 65 Call attention to the boxes at the top of the page. The first contains additional words with **dge;** the second has a word with both the hard and the soft sounds of **g.** If appropriate you can mention two examples of words where the **e** is dropped when **ment** is added—*judgment* and *abridgment.*

Page 66–67 ## Review: Sentences with th, wh, ce, ci, ge, gi, dge

Additional Activities

Have students underline, circle, and box a maximum of three sounds they need help with.

Page 68   **Special Skill: Previewing Words of Three or More Syllables from Story 4**

This lesson will prepare students to read *Justice Comes to Ridgeton* with relative ease. All the other words in the story have been recently learned or follow known rules. Since the words on this page are longer, the rules may be more difficult to interpret, but they are there. Because the words are broken into syllables, students will be able to see that they can pronounce them by putting the syllables together.

Read each word in syllables, then have students repeat after you. Then read the whole word, with students chorusing it. For example, **a—gen—da; agenda.**

When you dictate for the *Listen and write*, use whole words only.

Pages 69–72   **Story 4: Justice Comes to Ridgeton**

This story consolidates the sounds and skills learned in the second half of Chapter 3 *(th, wh, ce, ci, ge, gi, dge)*. It also includes selections from previous chapters and from Book One to reinforce learning.

Note
Phonetic specifications are listed after the story. If appropriate for your students, you might want to read this information to them.

Additional Activities

Have students mark (underline, circle, box, highlight) the new sounds *th, wh, ce, ci, ge, gi, dge.*

Discussion Questions

Select from the following questions those that are appropriate for your class; ask other questions. Encourage students to respond, to give their answers and opinions, and to ask additional questions. This will help them comprehend the information in the story and gain confidence in their growing abilities.

Note
Explain: *get the gist of* = to understand; *get with it* = to take steps to do something that must be done. (See Appendix D.)

Paragraph 1: What does *on the bench* mean? *(The judge is in court.)* Is the court secret or is it open to the public? *(open to the public)* Who is coming to Ridgeton today? *(Judge Alice G. Dodge)* Who wants to see the judge and the court in session? *(the public, citizens, college students)*

Paragraph 2: What are the "cops" doing? *(They are at vigil at the edge of the mob.)* What do they have? *(badges and guns)* What's in the cops' office? *(cells; a cabinet with a big lock; racks of guns, boxes of bullets, cuffs for felons)* (NOTE: Explain that *cops* is another word for "police." Discourage students from assuming that all cops are male.)

Paragraph 3: What is a gavel? *(a small wooden mallet)* What is a docket? *(a list of cases to be tried in court)* What is a witness? *(a person who says he or she saw something happen)* Who are the "12 men and women"? *(the jury)* (NOTE: *Jury* is a Book Three sound word.) What is the "box"? *(the area where the jury sits)*

(NOTE: At this point, it is very important to emphasize the role of the jury as well as that of the judge. In most trials in the United States, the jury determines the guilt or innocence of the accused, and the judge presides over the trial, explains the law to the jury, and determines the sentence, if any, to be passed on the accused. The jury is made up of ordinary people, representing a cross section of the population, to assure that the accused is tried by his or her peers, a right guaranteed in the Constitution to protect the people from the tyranny of a dictator. The jury plays a fundamentally important role in American justice. In this story we have emphasized the role of the judge, since *judge* is a sound word, but the reader should not infer a lack of importance of the jury.)

Paragraph 4: What is a felon? *(someone accused of a serious crime—a felony—such as burglary, kidnapping, murder)* What is an agenda? *(a written list of things or people to be dealt with)* What are the five cases on today's docket? *(See list in text.)* What is whiplash? *(a neck injury caused by a sudden jolt that snaps the head backward, then forward; can occur in car accidents)* What is ransom? *(price demanded by a kidnapper to free captive)* (NOTE: You might want to introduce the word *testify*, which is taught in Book Three, and explain that it means to give evidence in court.)

Paragraphs 5–10: Case #1. What does *allege* mean? *(to state positively, but without offering complete proof)* (NOTE: Tell students that this is very important. In U.S. courts, a person is considered innocent until proven guilty.) What are Beth and Rick accused of doing? *(tossing rocks at a bus)* What does Judge Dodge sentence them to? *(work at the Ridgeton Kids' Lodge to help younger, possibly needier children; play chess; do math; fence; dance)* What does the judge tell Mr. and Mrs. Hodge to do? *(discuss things with the kids; give them things to do; do things with them)* Are Rick and Beth willing to do what the judge requests? *(yes)* (NOTE: You may want to bring up the concept of "generation gap" with your class. This usually refers to children and parents having trouble communicating with each other. If appropriate, add that this is a "Western" concept. If your students are interested, discuss this issue with them. Ask how they are handling this in their own families.)

Paragraphs 11–13: Case #2. What is Chuck Cecil accused of? *(picking the lock on a hatchback)* Was there a witness? *(yes, Linda Chen)* What sentence does Judge Dodge give Chuck Cecil? *(30 days in a cell)* Can Mr. Cecil lighten his sentence? How? (Encourage discussion of the kinds of civic jobs Mr. Cecil might do to benefit others. If necessary, suggest hospital volunteer work, helping the elderly, etc.)

Paragraphs 14–18: Case #3. What are Gemma Conrad and Butch Sedgewick accused of? *(robbing Whitman's Gem Shop)* Do Butch and Gemma want to work for a living? *(no)* What do they want to do? *("fence" gems—to sell stolen goods for a "quick buck"—money)* What is a "chick"? *(in this case, a girlfriend)* How many witnesses were there? *(three)* What did they allege? *(that Butch and Gemma did rob Whitman's)* Are Gemma and Butch guilty? How do you know? *(yes; they confessed)* What sentence does Judge Dodge give Butch? *(11 months in a cell)* Gemma? *(15 months in a cell)* How can Gemma reduce her sentence? *(give back the 10-carat gem)* Will she do it? *(yes)* (NOTE: Explain that "rock" is slang for a jewel or a gem.)

Paragraphs 19–22: Case #4. What is Thelma Lodge accused of? *(reckless driving; hitting Lance Gillett's van)* What problem does Mr. Gillett have now because of the accident? *(whiplash)* What does Mrs. Lodge have to do for Mr. Gillett? *(give him a check for his losses)* Will Thelma Lodge do this? *(yes)*

Paragraphs 23–29: Case #5. What is a hit man? *(a hired killer)* What did Mad Max do? *(kidnapped and killed Cedric Whelton, even though he collected ransom)* What are henchmen? *(supporters/helpers—in this case, men and women who worked with Mad Max)* Was Mad Max repentant (regretful, sorry for what he did)?

(No, he's filled with malice; he wants to harm others.) Will the judge sentence him today? *(yes)* What does *sock it to him* mean? *(to give him the maximum sentence)* Does Mack Maxwell get the minimum or the maximum sentence? *(maximum)* How do you think Mad Max feels? *(very angry, maybe stunned that anyone would dare pass such a severe sentence on him)*

General Questions

1. What do you think of justice in Ridgeton?

2. What does justice mean to you—fairness, rightness, getting even, revenge, punishment, rehabilitation?

3. Discuss each case: Did _____ get justice? Why? Why not? If you were the judge, what would you have done?

Additional Activities
Have students underline **ge, dge, gi** words; circle **ce, ci** words; box **th, wh** words.

Chapter 4: Blends

Complete this chapter following the suggestions in "How to Use the Major Teaching Devices" and "How to Use the Major Text Sections" on pages 58–67 of this manual. Variations are noted below.

Pages 74–75   ## Initial Blends with l
Say:

In the special sounds you've been learning, the letters combined to make one new sound. For example, in **sh, s + h** became **sh.** You don't hear the **s (suh)** or the **h (huh)** alone anymore. Now you will learn a different way of combining sounds called *blends*. In a blend, two letters (consonants) keep their sounds, but come very close together. As an example, say *flag* and write the word on the board.

Tell students that in the word *flag*, you can hear the **f** and the **l**. Emphasize that the *f* and *l* sounds are not lost and not changed.

The blends are presented in vowel order. Read first the vowel sounds *ă, ĕ, ĭ, ŏ, ŭ* with the class, then the vowel sounds with the starting sounds: *lă, lĕ, lĭ, lŏ, lŭ.* Point to the third line and say *buh lă, buh lĕ, buh lĭ, buh lŏ, buh lŭ,* and have students repeat the sounds after you. Now point to the last line, and run the consonant sounds together quickly: *blă, blĕ, blĭ, blŏ, blŭ.* Help students practice all of the new blends introduced on pages 74 and 75 in the same way.

> **Note**
> Some students may have trouble with the sounds of **l** and **r**. They can say **la,** but when they add the **b,** it frequently becomes **bra.** Have them concentrate on **la,** just adding *buh* at the beginning. Reassure these students that a lot of practice is needed.

Pages 76–77   ## More Initial Blends with l (Including Special Endings ck, sh, ch, tch, th, wh, ce, ci, ge, gi, dge)
Read and break the blend into its two consonants if students have pronunciation problems; for example, *blab = b la b.*

Page 78   ## Sentences: Initial Blends with l

Additional Activity
Have students underline words containing blends with **l.**

Pages 79–80   ## Initial Blends with r
Follow the strategies described for pages 74–75.

Pages 81–82   **More Initial Blends with r (Including Special Endings: ck, sh, ch, tch, th, wh, ce, ci, ge, gi, dge)**

Follow the strategies described for pages 74–75.

Page 83   **Sentences: Initial Blends with r**

Follow the strategies used on pages 74–78, Initial Blends with **l**. Emphasize **r**. Same **l, r** reversal in pronunciation. Treat as noted on text page 74.

Pages 84–85   **Other Initial Blends: sc, sk, sm, sn, sp, st, sw, tw**

Follow the strategies described for pages 74–75.

Page 86   **Other Initial Blends (Including Special Endings: ck, sh, ch, tch, th, wh, ce, ci, ge, gi, dge)**

Follow the strategies described for pages 74–75.

Page 87   **Sentences: Other Initial Blends**

Additional Activity

Have students underline all the blends.

Page 88   **Special Skill: Previewing Words of Three or More Syllables from Story 5**

This lesson will prepare students to read *The Drop-In Clinic* with relative ease. All the other words in the story have been recently learned or follow known rules. Since the words on this page are longer, the rules may be more difficult to interpret, but they are there. Because the words are broken into syllables, students will be able to see that they can pronounce them by putting the syllables together.

Read each word in syllables, then have students repeat after you. Then read the whole word, with students chorusing it. For example, **ben—e—fit; benefit.**

When you dictate for the *Listen and write,* use whole words only.

Pages 89–91   **Story 5: The Drop-In Clinic**

This story consolidates the sounds and skills learned in the first part of Chapter 4 (Initial Blends). It also includes selections from previous chapters and from Book One to reinforce learning.

> **Note**
> Phonetic specifications are listed after the story. If appropriate for your students, you might want to read this information to them.

Additional Activity

Have students underline the initial blends.

Discussion Questions

Select from the following questions those that are appropriate for your class; ask other questions. Encourage students to respond, to give their answers and opinions, and to ask additional questions. This will help them comprehend the information in the story and gain confidence in their growing abilities.

Paragraph 1: What is a drop-in clinic? *(a clinic where no appointment or advance planning is necessary)* What is a clinic? *(usually a medical outpatient facility)* What are slick tricks? *(things done as if by magic; easy answers to hard questions that don't usually work)*

Paragraph 2: How do you pay at the clinic? *(credit plan, check, maybe medical insurance)* (NOTE: If appropriate for your students, ask if they have a clinic to go to? Is it "drop-in"?)

Paragraph 3: What is a checkup? *(a general physical exam)* What is a shot? *(an injection to produce immunity to diseases such as polio, smallpox, diphtheria, etc.)*

Paragraph 4: What is a regimen? *(a systematic plan, as of exercise and diet, usually to improve health)* What is a skin doctor called? *(a dermatologist)* (NOTE: Teach this and other terms as sight words.)

Paragraph 5: What part of a clinic would treat cuts and stabs? *(Emergency Room; Trauma Center)*

Paragraph 6: Do clinics have fitness centers? *(Usually not in the medical building. Fitness centers are generally private businesses. People who work for large corporations may have fitness centers on the premises.)*

Paragraph 7: What are some fitness activities? *(swimming, walking, jogging, biking)*

Paragraph 8: Dr. Twitchell recommends food to eat. Is she a dietician, a nutritionist, or a sports doctor? *(Dieticians usually are not medical doctors. She might be a Ph.D., also called "doctor.")* What should you eat for fitness and health? What foods should you avoid? *(See text.)*

Paragraph 9: What kind of doctor is Brad Clifton? *(an orthopedist, a bone specialist)*

Paragraph 11: Are drugs a big problem in your neighborhood? What can be done? *(Encourage discussion.)*

Paragraph 12: If someone has a lot of bad days, is glum, or feels blue, is this person happy or sad? *(sad)* What is depression? *(Sadness, low spirits for long periods of time. Many people have short periods—a few hours or a day here or there—when they may feel sad. With depression, however, the sadness goes on and on. For this medical condition, people can seek help (at a clinic) from a psychiatrist, a psychologist, or a social worker.)*

Paragraph 13: Can a Drop-In Clinic help someone? Do you have a clinic that helps?

Pages 92–98   Introduction to Final Blends

Explain that final blends are like initial blends, except that final blends come at the ends of words. Follow the directions on page 92 of the text.

Page 98   *Listen and write:* Dictate whole words. Start with one or two from each group.

Pages 99–100   ## Sentences: Final Blends

Additional Activity
Have students underline the final blends in the sentences.

Page 101   ## Special Skill: Previewing Words of Three or More Syllables from Story 6

This lesson will prepare students to read *Camp West Wind* with relative ease. All the other words in the story have been recently learned or follow known rules. Since the words on this page are longer, the rules may be more difficult to interpret, but they are there. Because the words are broken into syllables, students will be able to see that they can pronounce them by putting the syllables together.

Read each word in syllables, then have students repeat after you. Then read the whole word, with students chorusing it. For example, **cat—a—ma—ran; cata-maran.**

When you dictate for the *Listen and write,* use whole words only.

Pages 102–103   ## Story 6: Camp West Wind

This story consolidates the sounds and skills learned in the second part of Chapter 4 (Final Blends). It also includes selections from previous chapters and from Book One to reinforce learning.

> **Note**
> Phonetic specifications are listed after the story. If appropriate for your students, you might want to read this information to them.

Additional Activity
Have students underline the final blends.

Discussion Questions
Select from the following questions those that are appropriate for your class; ask other questions. Encourage students to respond, to give their answers and opinions, and to ask additional questions. This will help them comprehend the information in the story and gain confidence in their growing abilities.

Paragraph 1: Where is Camp West Wind? *(in Tampa, Florida, Southeastern United States)* (NOTE: If possible, point to this area on a map. Ask: What is the climate there? Does it snow in the winter? *not usually*) Who is Camp West Wind for? *(adults and children)*

Paragraph 2: What activities can you participate in at the camp? *(crafts, golf, tennis, track; tossing javelin and discus; running and jumping; swimming; resting; basking; hunting for shells)*

Paragraph 3: What is a raft? *(logs or boards fastened together to make a floating platform)* What is a catamaran? *(a boat with two hulls fitted together)* What is the helm? *(the steering wheel of a boat)* What does *aft* mean? *(toward the rear, or stern, of a ship)* What is a contestant? *(a person who participates in a contest)* What kind of vest must someone on a boat wear? *(a life vest)*

Paragraph 4: Is fishing allowed at the camp? *(yes)* Is hunting allowed? *(no)* What is a habitat? *(a protected place, a sanctuary, for animals, where no hunting is allowed)* What animals live in the habitat? *(muskrats, ducks, frogs, robins, insects)*

What is musk? *(a strong odor given off by animals such as muskrats and deer; used to make perfume)*

Paragraph 5: Is there a babysitter for infants at the camp? *(yes)* What does she do? *(gives infants milk, lunch, snacks, lots of rest)*

Paragraph 6: At night, what are some activities? *(a band, plays)* Describe the play. Who were the main characters? *(See text.)*

Paragraph 7: Epilog (an ending note after a story, play, or poem). Are the Lunds rich? *(Probably; they certainly are benefactors, people who give money to good causes.)* (NOTE: Explain that "yesterday" in this case means long ago, in the past.)

General Questions

1. Have you ever been to Florida? On a vacation?

2. Do you know any children who have gone to camp?

3. Have you ever been fishing? boating? swimming? Have you gone to a beach or a lake?

Pages 104–105

Review: Initial and Final Blends

Point out that the words on these two pages have blends at the beginning and the end.

Page 106

Review: Two-Syllable Words with Initial and Final Blends and the Special Sounds *ck, sh, ch, tch, th, wh, ce, ci, ge, gi, dge*

Additional Activity
Have students underline only the blends that seem to be causing difficulty.

Pages 107–108

Review: Sentences Using Words with Initial and Final Blends

Additional Activities
Have students underline only the blends that seem to be causing difficulty.

Page 109

Special Skill: Previewing Words of Three or More Syllables from Story 7

This lesson will prepare students to read *Trent's Dress and Pants Shop* with relative ease. All the other words in the story have been recently learned or follow known rules. Since the words on this page are longer, the rules may be more difficult to interpret, but they are there. Because the words are broken into syllables, students will be able to see that they can pronounce them by putting the syllables together.

Read each word in syllables, then have students repeat after you. Then read the whole word, with students chorusing it. For example, **ban—dan—nas; bandan-nas.**

When you dictate for the *Listen and write,* use whole words only.

Pages 110–113   ## Story 6: Trent's Dress and Pants Shop

This story consolidates the sounds and skills learned in the third part of Chapter 4 (Initial and Final Blends). It also includes selections from previous chapters and from Book One to reinforce learning.

Note

Phonetic specifications are listed after the story. If appropriate for your students, you might want to read this information to them.

Additional Activity

Have students underline the initial blends and circle the final blends.

Discussion Questions

Select from the following questions those that are appropriate for your class; ask other questions. Encourage students to respond, to give their answers and opinions, and to ask additional questions. This will help them comprehend the information in the story and gain confidence in their growing abilities.

Paragraph 1: **The Catalog.** What is a catalog? *(in this case, a paperbound booklet with pictures and prices of items for sale)* (NOTE: Ask if students have received catalogs in the mail. Would they buy something sight unseen from a catalog? How can the item be returned? If possible, bring in catalogs from local department stores or mail-order houses for students to look at. As an additional activity, consider reviewing how to fill out the mail-order form, including tax, postage, and handling. Explain that "handling charges" cover the costs of finding and packing the item.) What does Trent's sell? *(dresses, pants, prom dresses, swim trunks, golf pants, etc.)* Do you have to go to the store, or can you order in another way? *(don't have to go to the store; can order through the catalog by mailing or phoning in orders)*

Paragraph 2: Does Trent's have a wide variety of styles? *(yes)* Of what? *(dresses and pants)*

Paragraph 3: Do you have to be rich to shop at Trent's? *(no)*

Paragraph 4: **Fabrics.** What are fabrics? *(cloth used to make clothes)* What kind of fabrics can you find at Trent's? *(See text.)* What countries are they from? *(See text.)* (NOTE: If possible, bring in some pieces or swatches of cloth for students to feel and identify. Fabric stores sometimes have little pieces of material they may be willing to donate.)

Paragraph 5: **Prom Dresses.** What is a prom? *(usually a high school or college dance celebrating upcoming graduation; students dress up in gowns and tuxedos)* What kinds of prom dresses does Trent's sell? *(See text.)*

Paragraph 6: **Classic Day Dresses.** What are day dresses? *(dresses worn during the day)* What does *classic* mean? *(fine quality, simple design, stays in style a long time; not a fad—something that is in fashion for a short time and that people tire of quickly)* (NOTE: You may want to discuss with students what items they consider fads, e.g., miniskirts, felt skirts. Ask them what they think are classics.) What is a print? *(a fabric with a pattern)* What is a solid? *(fabric with no pattern, one solid color)*

Paragraph 7: **Extra Things.** What is a smock? *(a loose, lightweight jacket worn to protect clothing)* What is a kilt? *(a pleated skirt that reaches to the top of the knees; worn today on special occasions by men in Scotland)* What is a clan? *(in general, a group of people with similar interests and goals; in Scotland, a family* *group descended from the same ancestor)* (NOTE: Explain: studs are small removable buttons (of gold, silver, pearl, etc.) for men's dress shirts; white ducks are heavy cloth trousers; chaps are strong leather leggings worn over trousers (as protection) by cowhands; an ascot is a broad scarf looped under the chin; a cravat is a necktie.)

Paragraph 8: **The Loft.** What are the eight steps that go into making a dress at Trent's? Name the people and the step each one does. *(See text.)*

Paragraph 9: **A Problem in the Loft.** What is the problem in the loft? *(The boss on the second shift is unpleasant, unfair, and unprofessional.)* What does he do that the workers don't like? *(See text.)*

Paragraph 10: What does *do not bug us* mean? *(Don't bother us. See Appendix D.)* What does *picket* mean? *(In this context, it means workers striking—not working because of some grievance—usually peacefully walking back and forth with protest signs outside of the company.)*

Paragraph 11–13: **Models.** Where does the model show the dresses? *(in a tent)* What is she wearing? *(a trim jacket dress)* How does she move? *(She flits and prances; she doesn't slump or flush; she stands and doesn't twitch.)*

Paragraph 14: **The Custom Shop.** What happens in the Custom Shop? *(Clothes are fitted; alterations are made.)* What kinds of things can Bridget and Clem do? *(See text.)*

Paragraph 15: **Come to Trent's Today!** Does Trent's have what you want?

General Questions

1. Have you ever worked in a shop like Trent's? What did you do? What was your boss like?

2. Does Trent's remind you of a shop you know?

Pages 114–115   ## Bonus Page: Short-Vowel Words with Three or More Syllables Including Blends and Special Sounds

See "How to Use the *Bonus* Pages" on page 64 of this manual.

Page 116   ## Bonus Page: Sentences Using Short-Vowel Words with Three or More Syllables Including Blends and Special Sounds

See "How to Use the *Bonus* Pages" on page 64 of this manual.

Page 117   ## Bonus Page: Pronouncing Words with Three-Consonant Blends

Point out the initial three consonants in the words. For example, see *sprig.* Explain that students need to say the first two consonants together *(sp),* then the third consonant with the vowel *(ri),* followed by the final sound *(g):* **sp—ri—g.** (NOTE: Tell students that although the ninth item, **fifth,** is not a three-consonant blend (technically, *th* is a special sound), there are three consonants in a row. Have them treat this word like the three-consonant blends: **fif—th** = *fifth.*)

Chapter 5: Other Word Endings

Read down the list of new material to be learned in this chapter. Reassure students that each new concept will be taught individually, one step at a time. Explain that they already know some of the sounds and words from previous chapters and from Book One, and that they will be building on this knowledge. Add that the format of the pages will be the same as in earlier chapters.

Complete this chapter following the suggestions in "How to Use the Major Teaching Devices" and "How to Use the Major Text Sections" on pages 58–67 of this manual. Variations are noted below.

Page 120

Sound: *le*

Explain that **le** sounds like the end of the word *pull (uhl),* as in *candle,* not *lĕ.*

Page 121

Sentences Using Words with the le Ending

Additional Activity
Have students underline the **le** words.

Page 122

Sound: *al*

Explain that **al** sounds like the end of the word *pull (uhl),* as in *signal,* not *al* in *Allan, pal.* (Point out that it is the same sound as *le* in the previous lesson.)

Page 123

Sentences Using Words with the al Ending

Additional Activity
Have students underline the **al** words.

Page 124

Sound: *y*

Explain that **y** $= \bar{e}$ as in **he,** not like *yuh* in *yellow.*

Page 125

Sentences Using Words with the y Ending

Additional Activity
Have students underline the **y**-ending words.

> **Note**
> Call attention to the word *yummy* in the *Additional words* box, and point out that it has two kinds of **y**: **y** = *yuh* (the first **y**); **y** = $\bar{e}$ (the second **y**).

When the sentences are read, call attention to the **y** = *yuh* words—*yesterday* and *yummy* in item 5, and *you* in item 6. Have students circle those **y**'s.

Page 126

Sound: *ly*

Explain that **ly** = *lee,* as in *chilly, sadly.*

Page 127 ## Sentences Using Words with the ly Ending

Additional Activity
Have students underline the **ly** words in the sentences.

Page 128 ## Review: Words with le, al, y, ly

Compare: Emphasize the different sounds of the endings: *candle, candy.* Point out that the two words on each line are the same, except for their endings (for example: *gentle, gently; dismal, dismally).* You may want to write a few pairs on the board for students to compare and contrast.

Pages 129–130 ## Review: Sentences Using Words with le, al, y, ly

Additional Activities
Have students underline the words ending in **le** and **al,** circle the words ending in **y,** and box the words ending in **ly.**

Pages 131–132 ## Special Skill: Previewing Words of Three or More Syllables from Story 8

This lesson will prepare students to read *The Dance Academy's Festival* with relative ease. All the other words in the story have been recently learned or follow known rules. Since the words on this page are longer, the rules may be more difficult to interpret, but they are there. Because the words are broken into syllables, students will be able to see that they can pronounce them by putting the syllables together.

Read each word in syllables, then have students repeat after you. Then read the whole word, with students chorusing it. For example **a—cad—e—my; academy.**

When you dictate for the *Listen and write,* use whole words only.

Pages 133–134 ## Story 8: The Dance Academy's Festival

This story consolidates the sounds and skills learned in the first part of Chapter 5 (words ending in **le, al, y, ly**). It also includes selections from previous chapters and from Book One to reinforce learning.

> **Note**
> Phonetic specifications are listed after the story. If appropriate for your students, you might want to read this information to them.

Additional Activity
Have students underline the words ending in **le, al, y, ly.**

Discussion Questions
Select from the following questions those that are appropriate for your class; ask other questions. Encourage students to respond, to give their answers and opinions, and to ask additional questions. This will help them comprehend the information in the story and gain confidence in their growing abilities.

Paragraph 1: What is an academy? *(a school; a dance academy—a school for learning dancing)* What is a festival? *(a big party)* (NOTE: *party* is a sight word, taught in Book Three.) What is a potluck? *(in this case, lots of different kinds of food brought by the guests)* What is a brunch? (brunch *blends two words*—breakfast and lunch—*and means a meal eaten in the late morning that includes both breakfast and lunch foods.)* What does *She is as jumpy as can be* mean? *(She's nervous, worried.)* Why is Peggy Kimble jumpy? *(She has the major responsibility for organizing a dance festival.)*

Paragraph 2: What is the weather like on the day of the festival? *(It's dismal; it's chilly, foggy, and misty; it's drizzling.)* Does the weather matter to the guests? *(no)*

Paragraph 3: How is the academy decorated? *(It's dimly lit with candles; red and green holly and bottlebrush plants are on the mantel.)*

Paragraph 4: What did people bring to eat at the potluck? *(See text.)*

Paragraph 5: Is the music live or is it recorded or taped? *(live—a dance band)* What kind of music can the band play? *(See text.)*

Paragraph 6: What dances do the guests do? *(lindy, bunny hop, Mexican hat dance, belly dance, hully gully, shimmy, fox trot)* (NOTE: If appropriate for your students, either you or volunteers might demonstrate how to do some of these dances. The public library might have dance records or tapes.)

Paragraph 7: How does Henry sit? *(primly, timidly, stiffly)* Why doesn't Henry dance? *(He says he cannot.)* Who gets Henry to dance? *(Nelly)* How? *(She offers to help him and show him how to do it.)*

Paragraph 9: What happens at midnight? *(The festival ends; some guests help Peggy clean up; everyone thanks Peggy for her hospitality.)*

General Questions

1. Do you like to dance? Where do you dance? What dances do you like best?

2. Have you ever gone to a potluck supper? Did you bring food? What did you bring?

3. Have you ever gone to a party or festival where people were dancing? What was the occasion? *(wedding, birthday, graduation, etc.)*

Page 135 ## Sound: *ing*

Emphasize the nasal quality of **ng**. Explain that the *ng* sound comes "through the nose." Make sure students understand that **ng** does not sound like **nig** or **inguh**, but *ing* as in *ring, sing, wing.*

Page 136 ## Sentences Using ing Nouns

Additional Activity

Have students underline the words that end with **ing.**
NOTE: Call attention to the two sight words *nothing* and *something*. Point out that in these words, **o** = **ŭ** as in *sun.*

Pages 137–139 ## Adding ing to Verbs

Complete this lesson, following the directions on text page 137. Have students echo the words and word parts after you read them. For example: *pack (pack); ing (ing); packing (packing).*

For the *Listen and write* section, select and dictate whole words.

Page 140 ## Doubling a Consonant to Form ing Verbs

Explain that although an extra consonant is added in spelling, it is not pronounced as a syllable: not *ruh—nuh—ing,* but *run—ning.* You may want to remind students that they learned about doubling consonants in Book One.

Page 141 ## Adding ing to Verbs with *to be*

Read the three boxes at the top of the page, or have students read them. Explain that the **ing** form of the verb follows a form of *to be:* I am *(to be* form) packing (**ing** form of verb).

Tell students that the **ing** form stays the same for all people; the form of *to be* changes. They should use either *pack/packs* alone, or use a form of *to be* and *packing.*

Point out the somewhat different meanings:

• I pack every day. (general description)

• Today I am packing. (specific description, ongoing activity)

Page 142 ## Sentences Using ing Verbs

Additional Activity

Have students underline the words that end in **ing.** Contrast the sounds in item 2— *ink* and *ing* (see page 152); and item 3—*robin* sounds different from **ing.**

Page 143 ## Special Skill: Adding ing to Verbs

Follow the directions on text page 143. You may want to point out that students already know the words on this page.
Answer key:

1. canning	7. shutting
2. fitting	8. packing
3. shelling	9. fishing
4. shipping	10. chopping
5. filling	11. going
6. stitching	12. winning

NOTE: Point out that *going* in item 11 has no middle consonant.

Page 144 ## Sound: *ang*

Explain that *ang* has a nasal sound like *ing,* not *an* (as in *and*) nor *ahnig,* but *ang* like *ing.*

Page 145 ## Sentences Using Words with ang

Contrast the sound in *animals* (#3), *band* (#4), *sadness* (#5), *branch* (#6).

Additional Activity

Have students underline the words with **ang.**

Page 146   ## Sound: *ong*

Explain that *ong* has a nasal sound like *ing* and *ang*, not *onig*.

Page 147   ## Sentences Using Words with ong

Contrast the sounds in item 4 *(on)*.

Additional Activity

Have students underline the words with **ong.**

Page 148   ## Sounds: *ung, eng*

Explain that *ung, eng* have nasal sounds like *ing, ang, ong,* not *unig, enig.*

Page 149   ## Sentences Using Words with ung, eng

Contrast the sounds in item 5 *(lunch)* and item 6 *(then)*.

Additional Activity

Have students underline the words with **ung** and **eng.**

Page 150   ## Review: Comparing *ing, ang, ong, ung, eng*

Read the headings across the top of the page: **ing, ang, ong, ung, eng,** then all five lines from left to right *(sing, sang, song, sung)*. Call attention to the differences.

Then read down each column *(sing, Bing, Ling, mingle, string, tingle)*, calling attention to the similarities.

Have students write the words in the appropriate columns. Be sure they understand that all they have to do is copy the charts above.

For *Listen and write*, dictate down each column. Mix up the order only within a column. For example, dictate: *Ling, tingle, sing, . . .*

Page 151   ## Review: Sentences Using Words with ing, ang, ong, ung, eng

Additional Activity

Have students underline the words with **ng** groups.

Page 152   ## Sound: *ink*

Emphasize the nasal quality of *ink* (like *ing*). Tell students that they need to hear the **k** at the end *(inkuh),* but that it should be very soft.

Page 153   ## Sentences Using Words with ink

Contrast with *quick* in item 2.

Additional Activity

Have students underline the words with **ink.**

Page 154   ## Sound: *ank*

Emphasize the nasal quality of *ank* (like *ink)*. Remind students that they need to hear the **k**, but that it should be very soft.

Page 155   ## Sentences Using Words with ank

Contrast with *hand* in item 5.

Additional Activity
Have students underline the words with **ank.**

Page 156   ## Sound: *onk*

Emphasize the nasal quality of *onk* (like **ink, ank**). Remind students that they need to hear the **k,** but that it should be very soft.

Page 157   ## Sentences Using Words with onk

Contrast with *on* in item 3 and in item 6.

Additional Activity
Have students underline the words with **onk.**

Page 158   ## Sound: *unk, enk*

Emphasize the nasal quality of **unk, enk** (like **ink, ank, onk***).* Remind students that they need to hear the **k,** but that it should be very soft.

Page 159   ## Sentences Using Words with unk, enk

Contrast *bunk* and *Jenkins* in item 4 and *stuck* and *sunken* in item 6.

Additional Activity
Have students underline the words with **unk, enk.**

Page 160   ## Review: Comparing *ink, ank, onk, unk, enk*

Read the headings across the top of the page: **ink, ank, onk, unk, enk,** then all five lines from left to right *(clink, clank, clonk, clunk, Jenkins)*. Call attention to the differences.

Then read down each column *(clink, plink, sink, stink, drink, think)*, calling attention to the similarities.

Have students write the words in the appropriate columns. Be sure they understand that all they have to do is copy the charts above.

For *Listen and write,* dictate down each column. Mix up the order only within a column. For example, dictate: *drink, plink, think, . . .*

Pages 161–162   ## Review: Sentences Using Words with ink, ank, onk, unk, enk

Additional Activity
Have students underline the words with all **nk** groups.

Page 163   ## Special Skill: Previewing Words of Three or More Syllables from Story 9

This lesson will prepare students to read *The Franklin Fish Packing Plant* with relative ease. All the other words in the story have been recently learned or follow known rules. Since the words on this page are longer, the rules may be more difficult to interpret, but they are there. Because the words are broken into syllables, students will be able to see that they can pronounce them by putting the syllables together.

Read each word in syllables, then have students repeat after you. Then read the whole word, with students chorusing it. For example, **ben—e—fit—ing; bene-fiting.**

When you dictate for the *Listen and write,* use whole words only.

Page 163

Special Skill: Forming ing Words from le Words

Call attention to the special sound of **le** in the word *giggle.* Explain that the **le** sound *(uhl)* is dropped when *giggle (gig guhl)* becomes *giggling (gig gling),* not *gig guhl ing.* Have students echo the sounds after you say them.

When you dictate for *Listen and write,* use whole words only.

Page 164—166

Story 9: The Franklin Fish Packing Plant

This story consolidates the sounds and skills learned in the second part of Chapter 5 (words with **ing, ang, ong, ung, eng; ink, ank, onk, unk, enk**). It also includes selections from previous chapters and from Book One to reinforce learning.

> **Note**
> Phonetic specifications are listed after the story. If appropriate for your students, you might want to read this information to them.

Additional Activities
Have students underline the words with **ing, ang, ong, ung, eng** and circle the words with **ink, ank, onk, unk, enk** in the story.

Discussion Questions
Select from the following questions those that are appropriate for your class; ask other questions. Encourage students to respond, to give their answers and opinions, and to ask additional questions. This will help them comprehend the information in the story and gain confidence in their growing abilities.

Paragraph 1: What is a fish packing plant? *(a factory where fresh fish is cleaned, prepared, and packed)* What does Yung Chang do at the plant? *(See text.)* What is a checklist? *(in this case, a list of tasks that can be checked off as they are done)*

Paragraph 2: How does Yung feel about his job? *(He's glad to have it; his family has just come from Hong Kong.)*

Paragraph 3: What is Ingrid's job? *(shelling, bagging, tagging, packing fish)* What is Langston's job? *(in shipping; pushing a dolly—a movable platform for heavy objects; picking up sacks)*

Paragraph 4: What does Langston want to do on his day off? *(He wants his pal Yung to go on a fishing trip with him.)* What is a day off? *(time off from work; usually weekends and holidays)*

Paragraph 5: How does Yung feel about a fishing trip? *(He's not willing to go fishing; he doesn't want to be thinking of, smelling, or handling fish on a day off.)*

Paragraph 6: What is a hang-up? *(a problem about something; see Appendix D)*

Paragraph 7: What does Yung want Langston to help him with? *(tacking up some shingles on the shed)* Then what will they do? *(jogging, playing Ping-Pong)*

Paragraph 8: What does *ring you up* mean? *(call you on the phone)*

Paragraph 9: What do Linda and Hank King do? *(trucking)*

Paragraph 10: What is Inga Jenkins' job? *(canning fish; putting fish into a big black kettle to cook)* What is Stan's job? *(sticking tags on cans; stacking them in boxes)*

Paragraph 11: What is a shift? *(an eight-hour work period)* What is *punching the clock? (putting a time card into a time clock—when you arrive at work and when you go home—to record your starting and quitting times during one day)*

General Questions

1. Did you ever work in a factory or plant? What did the factory produce? What was your job?

2. Did you have friends at the factory? What did they do? What did the person next to you do?

3. Did you ever work on an assembly line? *(machines and workers through which parts of a product moved to be assembled)*

4. Did you ever punch a time clock?

Pages 167–180

The Three Different Sounds of ed: ed = ĭd; ed = d; ed = t

Explain that some verbs have a whole new word for their past-tense forms, for example, *sit, sat; do, did.* Reassure students that they know many of them already. Remind them of the chart on page 25 of present- and past-tense verbs without **ed** endings.

Have them turn to page 25 to review the words under the headings **Today** and **Yesterday.** You may want to list the past-tense forms under **Yesterday** on the board. Underline the verbs that change their form in the past tense: bid, *did,* fit, hit, quit, *had, ran, sat, got,* cut, *dug,* put, bet, let, set, wed, upset.

Page 167

Sound: ed = ĭd

Point out that students will be learning something different on page 167. The verbs on this page become past tense by adding **ed:** *land, landed; sift, sifted; blend, blended.*

Go on to explain that the **ed** ending has three different sounds: *ĭd* as in *landed; d* as in *filled; t* as in *jumped.* Tell the class that they will study each of these sounds separately, starting with **ed = ĭd.**

When reading, emphasize the **ed** as in *ĭd* sound.

Page 168

Special Skill: Spelling Words with the ed Ending

Complete this lesson, following the explanation in the text. Explain that all the words are pronounced in two syllables: landed *(lan—did);* matted *(mat—tid).*

Page 169   ## Sentences Using Words with ed = *ĭd*

Contrast with **ed** = *ĕd,* as in *Edwin* in item 1 and *Ned* in item 6.

Additional Activity

Have students underline the words with **ed** = *ĭd.*

Page 170   ## Sound: ed = *d*

Emphasize the *d* sound as in *filled* (*filld*), not *fill—ĭd.*

Page 171   ## Sentences Using Words with ed = *d*

Contrast with **ed** in *hedge* (*hege*), no *d* sound.

Additional Activity

Have students underline the words with **ed** = *d.*

Page 172   ## Sound: ed = *t*

Emphasize **ed** = *t* sound, as in *jumped* (*jumpt*), not *jumpĭd*, not *jumpd.*

Page 173   ## Sentences Using Words with ed = *t*

Additional Activity

Have students underline the words with **ed** = *t.*

Pages 174–175   ## Review: Sound Chart of Short-Vowel Words Ending in ed

Tell students that they will now review the three sounds of the **ed** ending: **ed** = *ĭd,* **ed** = *d,* **ed** = *t.* Point out that the *ĭd* sound is used for words whose root ends in **t** or **d.** (Make sure they note the **t** and **d** under the heading **Group Ending Sounds.**) Then point to the **t** and the **d** at the end of the root words *bat* and *add.*

Read Group 1: **ed** = *ĭd* sound. Read the pairs down the column: *bat, batted; pat, patted.*

Then read Group 2: **ed** = *d* sound. Read the pairs down: *enter, entered; banter, bantered.*

Last, read Group 3: **ed** = *t* sound pairs: *hop, hopped; help, helped.*

> **Note**
> Don't expect your students to learn the sounds of the root endings (**p, k, s,** etc.). But point them out to show that there is some linguistic reason for these different **ed** sounds.

Page 176   *Listen and write:* Dictate either all the same group or mixed groups. Announce your intentions to the class, saying:

I will dictate three words with the *ĭd* ending: *batted, patted, fitted.* Now I will dictate three words with the *d* ending: *slammed, jabbed, filled.* Finally, I will dictate three words with the *t* ending: *mixed, jumped, buffed.*

OR: I will dictate three words with different-sounding endings: *batted, hopped, entered.*

OR: Label the top of the columns on the *Listen and write* page with *ĭd, t,* and *d.* I will dictate some words with **ed** endings. Write them in the column that has the sound of the ending.   Then dictate *filled, chapped, lasted.* Students will put *filled* under *d, chapped* under *t,* and *lasted* under *ĭd.*

Page 177

Review: Short-Vowel Words Ending in ed

Answer key:

ed = ĭd	**ed = t**	**ed = d**
patted	helped	filled
flitted	shopped	lived
lasted	jumped	slammed
planted	packed	jabbed
melted	missed	begged
expected	danced	canned
invested	fixed*	studied**
butted	finished*	buzzed
padded	hatched*	whizzed
plodded	crunched*	entered
funded	buffed	
blended	hopped	

* Don't double the consonant.
****y** changes to **i** before **ed**

Additional Activities
Have students read aloud, taking turns. Read in order, down columns. Check for pronunciation. Then have them read across the rows. Finally, have them number the words (first column 1–17, second column 18–34), then call on individuals to read specific items by number.

Page 178   *Listen and write:* Dictate root word, then dictate word with **ed** ending. OR: Dictate five root words and have students write in the words with **ed** endings. (NOTE: This provides practice and reinforcement of skills; it is not a test.)

Page 179

Review: Sentences with Words Ending in ed
Contrast with *Ed* in *Edison* in item 5 (**ed = ĕd**).

Additional Activities
Have students underline all **ed** endings with *ĭd, t, d* sounds, or have them distinguish the sounds and underline *ĭd* sound, circle *t* sound, box *d* sound.

Page 180   *Listen and write:* Dictate whole sentences or phrases.

Pages 181–182

Special Skill: Previewing Words of Three or More Syllables from Story 10

This lesson will prepare students to read *We Visited Uncle Ned's Cattle Ranch* with relative ease. All the other words in the story have been recently learned or follow known rules. Since the words on this page are longer, the rules may be more difficult to interpret, but they are there. Because the words are broken into syllables, students will be able to see that they can pronounce them by putting the syllables together.

Read each word in syllables, then have students repeat after you. Then read the whole word, with students chorusing it. For example, **ac—com—plished; accomplished.**

When you dictate for the *Listen and write,* use whole words only. Provide additional paper, if necessary, so that students can copy or rewrite the words they had problems with.

Pages 183–186

Story 10: We Visited Uncle Ned's Cattle Ranch

This story consolidates the sounds and skills learned in the third part of Chapter 5 (**ed** past-tense ending with three different sounds—*ĭd, d, t*). It also includes selections from previous chapters and from Book One to reinforce learning.

> **Note**
> Phonetic specifications are listed after the story. If appropriate for your students, you might want to read this information to them.

Additional Activities

Have students underline the words with **ed** = *ĭd,* circle those with **ed** = *d,* and box those with **ed** = *t.*

> **Note**
> If appropriate for your class, explain that this story is a first-person narrative. This means that it is told from one person's point of view. Tell students to look for the pronoun *I* as they read. This is the clue. Ask them if they know who the person telling the story is. *(daughter/sister)* Is her name mentioned in the story? *(no)*

Discussion Questions

Select from the following questions those that are appropriate for your class; ask other questions. Encourage students to respond, to give their answers and opinions, and to ask additional questions. This will help them comprehend the information in the story and gain confidence in their growing abilities.

Paragraph 1: What is a split-level? *(a style of house in which the floor level of the rooms on one side is approximately halfway between the floor levels on the other side)* What does *invest* mean? *(to commit money to something in order to make a profit)* What did Uncle Ned do? *(invited them to visit his cattle ranch)* Where is Kansas? *(Midwest; if possible, show a map.)*

Paragraph 2: How did the family pay for the trip? *(budgeted—set aside money from regular income; cashed in some savings bonds)*

Paragraph 3: How did they travel and carry their luggage? *(They rented a van.)* What did they take? *(See text.)*

Paragraph 4: Was packing easy or difficult? *(difficult)* How long did it take? *(a full day)*

Paragraphs 5–10: Name the five things that happened while they were packing. *(See text.)*

Paragraph 11: What time did they go to bed? *(8 P.M.)* What time did they wake up? *(8 A.M.)* What does *cuffed his pants* mean? *(rolled up the bottoms slightly)* How do you know their house was closed up? *("It was locked up.")*

Paragraph 12: How long did it take to drive to the ranch? *(a full day)* Was the ranch big? *(yes)* How do you know? *(". . . went on and on.")* Where did the children sleep? *(bunked with the ranch hands)* Where did their parents sleep? *(lodged with Uncle Ned)*

Paragraph 13: What animals did Uncle Ned have? *(cattle, chickens, kids—baby goats—pigs and hogs, little chicks hatched from eggs)* List five things the family did with the animals. *(See text.)* (NOTE: Point out that the word *kid* is used in two ways—for baby goats in this paragraph and for children in paragraph 15.) What does *candle the eggs* mean? *(to hold between the eye and a light to test for staleness, fertility, etc.)*

Paragraph 14: What was the name of Uncle Ned's best bull? *(Teddy)* Describe Teddy. Was he dangerous? *(yes)* (NOTE: Explain that *Angus* is the name of a breed of bull.)

Paragraph 15: What did the children want to do? *(get on the bull)* What did they sneak into? *(the fenced-in ring)* What did Teddy do? *(got miffed; panted, huffed, and puffed)* What did the kids do? *(dashed from the bull; jumped the fence)* Did Uncle Ned punish them? *(no)* Why? *(He yelled, but he didn't punish them because they had been punished running in fear from a maddened bull.)*

Paragraph 16: List five tasks the children helped with. *(See text.)* What do these words mean—*tilled, mulched, threshed, hulled? (They are all terms related to clearing land and preparing wheat.)*

Paragraph 17: Where did the children camp with Uncle Ned and the ranch hands? *(grassland)* What is a chuck wagon? *(a wagon in which food is cooked and served. Remind students that they learned this term in an earlier story.)* What did the ranch hands do? *(fiddled—played the violin; sang ballads; gossiped and chatted)*

Paragraph 18: Was the visit to the ranch challenging for the family? *(yes)* Did they find it easy? *(no)* Was it worth it? *(yes)*

Paragraph 19: How did the family feel when they left the ranch? *(sad)* Did Uncle Ned say that they had helped him? *(yes)* Do you think they really did? *(yes)* Did the ranch hands like the family? *(yes)* Who benefited most from the visit—the family or Uncle Ned? Was Ned just being a "loving uncle"? *(Encourage discussion.)*

Page 187   Sound: *er*

Emphasize *er* (as in *her*), not *er* (as in *cherry, merry*).

Page 188   Sentences Using Words with er

Explain that **er** has several meanings. One meaning is a person or thing doing the action. For example:

action = *running;* person doing the action = *runner*

Draw a chart on the board. As students read the sentences, place the key words on the chart to show what the pairs of sentences indicate. Your chart should look something like this:

Action		Person Doing the Action	
1.	jump	jumper	Nick/He
2.	sand	sander	Beth/She
3.	drill	driller	Kevin/He
4.	pitch	pitcher	Donna/She
5.	run	runner	Chuck/He
6.	bat	batter	Anna/She

Page 189

Special Skill: er at the End of a Word = Noun

Explain that **er** at the end of a word = a common noun. Add that a common noun is one that names a general—not specific—person, place, or thing. These are examples of common nouns: *student* (person—refers to any student); *school* (place—refers to any school); *pencil* (thing—refers to any pencil).

Additional Activities

Words: Ask students to name a common noun for each category—person, place, and thing. Have a volunteer write the words on the board.

Sentences: Have students underline the **er** words in the sentences.

Page 190

Special Skill: er at the End of a Word = Adjective

Explain that an adjective is a word that tells something about a noun. An adjective answers one of these three questions: 1. What kind? 2. Which one? 3. How many?

Adjectives progress: *fat, fatter, fattest. Fatter* means more fat; *fattest* means the most fat of all. Tell students that in this lesson they will learn adjectives that end in **er.**

Note

Make students aware of the exceptions *good, better, best*. Help them understand that when something is more than just good, it becomes **better,** not "more good" or "gooder." Emphasize that there are no such words as "more good" or "gooder." If you want, add that the adjective **best** means "better than better," something nothing else can top. (*Good* will be taught in Book Three.)

Additional Activities

1. Have students underline the **er** words. (Point out that *yesterday* in item 2 is not an adjective. It doesn't tell what kind, although it has **er** and sounds the same.)

2. Have students create new sentences with the twelve adjectives at the top of the page.

3. Ask students to create three sentences, one with each of these adjectives: *good, better, best*.

Page 191   *Listen and write:* Dictate whole or partial sentences.

Page 192   ## Special Skill: Spelling Words with the er Ending

Emphasize that the spelling rule is similar to adding **ing** and **ed** to words. (You may want students to look back at text pages 137–140 and the **ed** chart on pages 174–175.)

In section B, point out that these words are pronounced in two syllables: *bat—ter = batter; win—ner = winner.*

Pages 193–194   ## Review: Chart of Words with er

Read the chart, moving down each column, then chain read around the room. Review the note at the bottom of page 194. Explain that some words have different uses, for example, *better,* which may be used as an adjective and as a verb. Other examples:

1. The candles *glimmer*. (verb)

2. We saw a *glimmer* from the candles. (noun)

1. *Center* the picture on the wall. (verb)

2. Do they go to the Senior *Center*? (noun)

3. Please give me the *center* chair. (adjective)

Page 195   *Write (or Listen and write):* If your students are comfortable with this skill, increase the quantity of words you dictate. OR: If your students are having difficulty handling these words, you may want to use this page for practicing writing. OR: Use half of the page for writing practice and the other half for *Listen and write*.

Pages 196–197   ## Review: Sentences with Three Kinds of er Words

Additional Activity

Have students underline the **er** words. Remind them to exclude *yesterday* in item 4.

Pages 198–201   ## Special Skill: Previewing Words of Three or More Syllables from Story 11

This lesson will prepare students to read *Mr. Webster's Day at the Bunker Hill Bank* with relative ease. All the other words in the story have been recently learned or follow known rules. Since the words on this page are longer, the rules may be more difficult to interpret, but they are there. Because the words are broken into syllables, students will be able to see that they can pronounce them by putting the syllables together.

Read each word in syllables, then have students repeat after you. Then read the whole word, with students chorusing it. For example, **ad—min—is—ters; administers.**

When you dictate for the *Listen and write,* use whole words only. Provide additional paper, if necessary, so that students can copy or rewrite the words they had problems with.

Pages 202–205

Story 11: Mr. Webster's Day at the Bunker Hill Bank

This story consolidates the sounds and skills learned in the last part of Chapter 5 (words ending in **er**). It also includes selections from previous chapters and from Book One to reinforce learning.

> **Note**
> Phonetic specifications are listed after the story. If appropriate for your students, you might want to read this information to them.

Additional Activity

Have students underline the words ending in **er.**

Discussion Questions

Select from the following questions those that are appropriate for your class; ask other questions. Encourage students to respond, to give their answers and opinions, and to ask additional questions. This will help them comprehend the information in the story and gain confidence in their growing abilities.

Paragraph 1: What was Robert Webster's job *(bank officer and manager)* Is he good at it? *(yes)* Do people respect him? *(yes)*

Paragraph 2: Is Robert married or single? *(single)* How do his parents feel about that? *(They want him to marry, but they don't badger him about it.)* What do his parents do? *(swim; golf; jog; keep a pet dog)* (NOTE: Mention that since Robert's parents have a lot of time for sports, they are probably retired.) Where do they live? *(On an island off Massachusetts; if possible, show students where Nantucket is on a map.)*

Paragraph 3: Do you think the Websters are rich? Why? *(Encourage discussion.)*

Paragraph 4: What do you think *were Emersons* means? *(The family may be related to Ralph Waldo Emerson (1803–1882), a great poet, writer, orator, and philosopher, who was born in Boston, Massachusetts.)*

Paragraph 5: What was the weather like on Monday? *(brisker and wetter than Sunday)* How was Robert dressed? *(He had a muffler under his slicker, and lavender suspenders under his gray flannel jacket.)*

Paragraph 6: What time did the bank open? *(at 8 A.M.)* When did Robert arrive? *(at 7:50 A.M.)* Who opened the doors? *(Chester Brenner and Hester Miller)* What are some of the services the Bunker Hill Bank provides? *(See text.)*

Paragraph 7: What is Beverly Anderson's job? *(trust officer)* Does Robert like Beverly? *(yes)* How can you tell? *("Beverly was wonderful.")* Does Beverly like Robert? *(yes)* How can you tell? *("She had a hankering for Robert.")*

Paragraph 8: Name Robert's customers, and tell what they want at the bank. *(See text.)*

Paragraph 9: Are the Gerbers young or old? *(old)* Do they like to travel? *(yes)* Where have they just been? *(Switzerland)* Where do they plan to go? *(Rochester to Denver, then Vermont)*

Paragraph 10: What do the Hendersons want to do in their business? *(expand)* Do they need a loan? *(yes)* For what? *(to buy tandem rigs)*

Paragraph 11: Why does Robert trust the Hendersons? *(See text.)*

Paragraph 12: Are Miss Polly and Miss Abby Vanderhoff rich? *(yes; well-to-do)* Are they married? *(no; spinsters)* What are fraternal twins? *(not identical)* What do they want to do to their home? *(convert the loft into an art center; fix up the gutters; put in a lift—elevator)* Why? *(loft is cluttered; Miss Polly isn't well)*

Paragraph 13: Is Miss Abby bossy? *(yes)*

Paragraph 14: Are the Vanderhoff sisters borrowing money? *(No, they're taking money out of their trust fund.)*

Paragraph 15: What did Dexter Skinner want? *(a letter of credit)* Is he a good credit risk? Why or why not? *(no; bad investments, bankrupt, tax problems, spendthrift)*

Paragraph 16: What does *gotten Skinner's number* mean? *(He saw him for what he really was—a gambler and a gangster. See Appendix D.)*

Paragraph 17: What did Robert invite Beverly to do? *(have dinner with him)*

Paragraph 18: What did Robert and Beverly have for dinner? *(salad, crackers, lobster, apple fritters with sherbet)* What did they do after dinner? *(danced, lingered at the club)* How does Robert feel about Beverly? *(He's "fonder of her than ever.")*

Paragraph 19: Do you think Robert will ask Beverly to marry him? *(maybe)* What is a *blockbuster? (in this case, a wonderful day, when everything went well)* (NOTE: Explain that the phrase *lived happily ever after* is a traditional ending to popular fairy tales, variations of which are found throughout the world.)

Chapter 6: Contractions and Special Sounds

Read down the list of new material to be learned in this chapter. Reassure students that each new concept will be taught individually, one at a time. Point out that they already know some of the sounds and words from previous chapters and from Book One, and that they will be building on this knowledge. The format of the pages follows a pattern similar to ones used before.

Complete this chapter following the suggestions in "How to Use the Major Teaching Devices" and "How to Use the Major Text Sections" on pages 58–67 of this manual. Variations are noted below.

Page 208
Contractions Using 's: it is = it's
Follow the instructions on the text page. Go over them with students. Write **it is = it's** on the board and explain that the apostrophe takes the place of the missing letter or letters. Point out that *contract* means to get smaller. Two words have formed one smaller word.

To make the contraction **it's:**

1. Drop the **i** from **is**   it i̸s

2. Add an apostrophe after **it** in place of the dropped **i**   it + ' + s

3. Squeeze the two words together   **it's**

Pages 209–211
Contractions Using 's: that's, *noun*'s, he's, she's, I'm
Tell students to follow the same steps to make the contractions: **that's** (that is); *noun*'s (noun is); **he's** (he is); **she's** (she is).

Point out that **I'm** (I am) differs only because this contraction uses **'m** instead of **'s.** But the steps are the same:

To make the contraction **I'm:**

1. Drop the **a** from **am**   I a̸m

2. Add an apostrophe after **I**   I + ' + m

3. Squeeze the two words together   **I'm**

> **Note**
> Remind students that *I* is always capitalized, even if it is part of a contraction, even in the middle of a sentence.

Pages 212–213
Contractions with not = n't: isn't, aren't, wasn't, weren't, hasn't, haven't, can't
Write on the board:

is not = isn't	has not = hasn't
are not = aren't	have not = haven't
was not = wasn't	cannot = can't*
were not = weren't	

To make contractions with **not:**

1. Drop the **o** from **not**   is noʈ

2. Replace it with an apostrophe   is n't

3. Squeeze the two words together   **isn't**

***Cannot** is already one word. To make the contraction **can't,** drop the **no** from **not,** then squeeze together: **can + ' + t = can't**

Page 213   *Listen and write:* Dictate sentences from pages 208–212. Use two from page 211, to include **I'm.**

Page 214   ## Review: Contractions with is; with not; and with am

At the top of the page, compare each contraction with the words from which it was made.
Answer key:
Contractions: isn't, can't, it's, weren't, she's, haven't, wasn't, the dog's, that's, aren't, hasn't, he's, I'm

    Full words: I am, were not, have not, she is, it is, cannot, has not, is not, was not, that is, the shopper is, are not, he is

Page 215   ## Bonus Page: Completing Sentences with Contractions

Make sure that students see that they can select the answers from the box at the top of the page.
Answer key:

1. weren't	6. Isn't	10. haven't
2. aren't	7. That's	11. He's
3. it's	8. can't	12. wasn't
4. Nancy's	9. She's	13. I'm
5. hasn't		

Page 216   ## Sound: y = ĭ

Explain that **y** = ĭ as in *inch,* not **y** = ē as in *happy,* not **y** = **yuh** as in *yellow, yam,* but **y** as in *gym, gypsum, cyst.*

Page 217   ## Sentences Using Words with the y = ĭ Sound

Call attention to the *Additional words* box and point out the list of words that have two sounds of **y** (the last column).
    In the sentences, contrast with **y** = ē in *mystery* (#4) and *tyranny* (#6).

Additional Activities
Have students underline the **y** = ĭ words only. Then ask them to circle the other **y** sounds in the words.

Page 218   Sound: *ive*

Explain that the **i** in *ive* sounds like the ĭ in *inch* and *give*.

Page 219   Sentences Using Words with the ive Ending

Additional Activity
Have students underline the **ive** = ĭv words.

Page 220   Sound: *tion*

Point out that **tion** sounds like **shun,** as in *addition*.

Page 221   Sentences Using Words with the tion Ending

Additional Activity
Have students underline the words with **tion.** Tell them to omit the word *question;* remind them that *question* sounds like **questyon.**

Pages 222–225   Special Skill: Previewing Words of Three or More Syllables from Story 12

This lesson will prepare students to read the newspaper-style article with relative ease. All the other words in the article have been recently learned or follow known rules. Since the words on this page are longer, the rules may be more difficult to interpret, but they are there. Because the words are broken into syllables, students will be able to see that they can pronounce them by putting the syllables together.

Read each word in syllables, then have students repeat after you. Then read the whole word, with students chorusing it. For example, **a—bys—mal; abysmal.**

When you dictate for the *Listen and write,* use whole words only. Provide additional paper, if necessary, so that students can copy or rewrite the words they had problems with.

Pages 226–227   Story 12: The Crystal Junction Banner

This newspaper-style article consolidates the sounds and skills learned in Chapter 6 (words with **y** = ĭ, **ive, tion,** and contractions). It also includes selections from previous chapters and from Book One to reinforce learning.

> **Note**
> Phonetic specifications are listed after the story. If appropriate for your students, you might want to read this information to them.

Additional Activities
Have students underline the words with **y** = ĭ, **ive, tion,** and circle the contractions in the story.

Pre-Reading Discussion

Explain that this story looks like a newspaper article. (You may want to bring in a newspaper to pass among students so they can compare it with the article in their text.)

Have students look over the article. Point out and discuss the following parts of a newspaper (source: *World Book Encyclopedia*). You may want to write these newspaper terms on the board.

1. *Masthead:* **The Crystal Junction Banner** The name of the newspaper as it is displayed on the front page of the paper. Other common names for newspapers are *Gazette, Times, Journal, Post, Dispatch, Bulletin, Tribune,* often combined with the name of a city or town. (NOTE: *masthead* also refers to a box containing the name of the paper, the publisher's name, and the names of the principal editors, which usually appears on the editorial page. If possible, display such a page from a local newspaper.)

2. *Edition:* **Wednesday, July 26, 1989** The issue, or date, of the paper.

3. *Headline:* **Member of Congress Flynn Running for Top Elective Office** The heading of an article. A *banner headline* is one that extends across the top of the page.

4. *Byline:* **Lynn Plympton** The name of the reporter who wrote the story. (NOTE: At the *Crystal Junction Banner*, Lynn Plympton is a staff reporter with a regular *beat*—she's assigned to cover political issues. When her article is of great public interest, or when she finds out facts before other newspapers do, it is considered a *scoop* or an *exclusive.*)

5. *Dateline:* **Crystal Junction**—Refers to the line at the beginning of a news article that tells where the story takes place.

6. *Lead:* **At the political convention held today . . .** Opening paragraph of a news story.

7. *Subhead:* **Citizens question Flynn** Short heading used to break up the paragraphs of a long article. (NOTE: Also point out the inserts in the article set off by lines, which are meant to draw readers' attention and highlight the main points of the story. There are two in this article.)

Other newspaper terms that might be of interest to students are:

8. *Deadline:* The due date, the time limit for preparing and publishing a particular edition of the paper.

9. *Copy:* Article being prepared to be set in type.

10. *Extra:* A special edition of the paper.

Discussion Questions

Select from the following questions those that are appropriate for your class; ask other questions. Encourage students to respond, to give their answers and opinions, and to ask additional questions. This will help them comprehend the information in the story and gain confidence in their growing abilities.

Paragraph 1: What is the name of the newspaper? *(The Crystal Junction Banner)*

Paragraph 2: What is the date of the edition? *(Wednesday, July 26, 1989)*

Paragraph 3: What does Flynn do now? *(member of Congress)* What does *running for office* mean? *(trying to get elected)* What does *campaigning* mean? *(making speeches, etc., to persuade people to vote for him)* What does *top elective office* mean? *(president)* Who wrote this article? *(Lynn Plympton)* What is her job? *(staff reporter)*

Paragraph 4: Where did Lyndon Flynn give his speech? City? Building? *(at a political convention at the Civic Center in Crystal Junction)*

Paragraph 5: What did Flynn talk about? *(his positions on political issues, also called a "platform" [Book Three])*

Paragraphs 6–17: What did he promise to do? (NOTE: Tell students that the dashes are a clue to finding the issues; there's a dash in front of each one.) (a slang term for the term *issues* is "planks" in the "platform")

Paragraph 18: How did the citizens react? (NOTE: Again, the dashes indicate the different reactions.)

Paragraph 19: What is a synopsis? *(a summary)*

Paragraph 27: What does *mudslinging* mean? *(saying offensive things about a political opponent)*

Paragraph 28: Will Gladys Dylan vote for Flynn? *(yes)*

Paragraph 29: What was the consensus (general agreement, opinion) of the people? *("Flynn's got strong convictions.")*

Paragraph 30: What is a national anthem? What is it in the United States? *(a song of praise, devotion, and patriotism about a country; In the United States, "The Star-Spangled Banner" is the official national anthem.)*

Appendices

There are six appendices, each with its own format. The skills summarized in them appear throughout Book Two. The material in the appendices can be used in a variety of ways:

1. To provide review material for students at the end of Book Two.

2. To provide reinforcement of the skills learned, and to show students how far they have advanced. (Point out how many names, places, idioms, and so on they can read and understand.)

3. To provide material to

   • generate sentences for *Listen and write*

   • offer additional practice

   • use as reference charts

Refer to the appendices as needed throughout the book.

Appendix A: Sight Words

Pages 230–232 contain sight words from Books One and Two. Review the sight words from Book One with students before completing Chapter 1.

Appendix B: Alphabetized List of Introductory Two-Syllable, Short-Vowel Words and Names

The two-syllable words from text pages 5 through 13 are alphabetized here. You may want to review alphabetization.

> **Note**
> This list is for your convenience. It will help you locate words for additional sentences.

Appendix C: Geography—Some Places with Short-Vowel Names

Emphasize how many important geographical terms students can read and pronounce, using short vowels. Point out that some post office-authorized two-letter state abbreviations are also listed.

Appendix D: Idioms

There are two sections:

• Part I lists the idioms used in Book Two. Their definitions and location in the book are also noted.

- Part II provides additional idioms that students are capable of reading, using the skills they develop in Book Two. Each idiom is presented with its definition, the phonetic element it illustrates, and the chapter in which the element is taught. You may want to ask students to create their own sentences, using these idioms.

Appendix E: Common Last Names with Short Vowels, y Endings, and Color Sight Words

Point out how many common last names with short vowels and special sounds students can read, using Book Two skills.

Appendix F: Summary of Sounds and Words in the Stories in Book Two

This appendix presents the sounds and words used in the stories, arranged in two charts:

Chart I: Phonetic elements and sight words

Chart II: Words and names of three or more syllables

In addition, the stories are listed by number, chapter, title, and phonetic elements and sight words emphasized.

To determine the content of a story, read up on the chart. A story emphasizes everything on its lines in the chart and includes selections from everything that came before.

Book Three

Book Three contains Units I–III with fifteen chapters, Appendices A–F, and seven stories.

Objectives of Book Three

Unit One: **Long Vowels**	Reviews short vowels Introduces long vowels
Chapter 1: **Introduction to Long Vowels**	Reviews Book Two words of two or more syllables with short vowels and special sounds Introduces long vowels as compared to short vowels
Chapter 2: **Long Vowels with Open Syllables**	Presents long vowels with open syllables: • at the end of words • inside words • in multisyllabic words • in prefixes • in contractions
Chapter 3: **Long Vowels with Silent e**	Presents the concept of silent **e** changing short vowels to long vowels, using the five long vowels with silent **e: a-e, e-e, i-e, o-e, u-e;** and *WORD ALERT* exceptions
Unit Two: **Long-Vowel Sounds Made From Other Letter Combinations**	Presents additional letter combinations that make the five long-vowel sounds, and *WORD ALERT* exceptions
Chapter 4: **The ā Sound**	Presents seven letter combinations that make the *ā* sound: **ai** *(rain);* **ay** *(hay);* **ange** *(danger);* **aste** *(paste);* **able** *(table);* **ey** *(they);* **ei** *(veil)*
Chapter 5: **The ē Sound**	Presents six letter combinations that make the *ē* sound: **ee** *(feet);* **ea** *(leaf);* **ie** *(field);* **ei** *(ceiling);* **y** *(city);* **i** *(ski)* Presents *WORD ALERT* exceptions **ea** = *ĕ (bread);* **ea** = *ā (steak)* Presents special sounds of **ea: i** = *yuh (petunia)*
Chapter 6: **The ī Sound**	Presents five letter combinations that make the *ī* sound: **y** *(fly);* **ie** *(tie);* **igh** *(light);* **ild** *(child);* **ind** *(find)*
Chapter 7: **The ō Sound**	Presents five letter combinations that make the *ō* sound: **oe** *(toe);* **oa** *(boat);* **ow** *(snow);* **ol** *(bolt);* **ost** *(post)*
Chapter 8: **The ū Sound**	Presents one letter combination that makes the *ū* sound: **ew** *(yew)*
Unit Three: **Special Sounds**	Presents letter combinations that make special sounds (not long or short vowels) and *WORD ALERT* exceptions

Chapter 9: **The $\overline{oo}$ Sound**	Presents five letter combinations that make the $\overline{oo}$ sound: **oo** *(moon);* **ew** *jewel);* **ue** *(glue);* **ui** *(fruit);* **ou** *(soup)* *Presents **WORD ALERT** exception* **oo** = $\breve{oo}$ *(foot)*
Chapter 10: **Other Sounds with o**	Presents four letter combinations that make other **o** sounds: **ow** = *ow (cow);* **ou** = *ow (house);* **oi** = *oi (coin);* **oy** = *oi (boy)* *Presents **WORD ALERT** exception* **ou** = *ŭ (country)*
Chapter 11: **r-Related Vowel Sounds**	Presents twelve letter combinations with **r** that make **r**-related sounds: *or (corn);* **er** and related sounds *er (computer),* *ir (bird),* *ur (nurse),* *ear (pearl),* *our (journal),* *wor (worm);* **ar** = *ar (car);* **air** and related sounds **air** = *air (chair),* **are** = *air (square),* **ary** = *airy (dictionary),* **ear** = *air (bear)*
Chapter 12: **aw and Related Sounds**	Presents seven letter combinations that make **aw**-related sounds: **aw** = *aw (saw),* **au** = *aw (saucer),* **all** = *awl (ball),* **al** = *awl (salt),* **alk** = *awk (chalk),* **qua** = *quaw (quarter),* **war** = *wor (warm)* *Presents **WORD ALERT** exceptions* **wa** = *wah (swan),* **qua** = *quah (squash)*
Chapter 13: **Special Consonant Sounds**	Presents: • two letter combinations that make the *f* sound: **ph** *(phone);* **gh** *(enough)* • five letter combinations that make the *sh* sound: **ci** *(commercial);* **ti** *(patient);* **s** *(sugar);* **sion** *(mission);* **tion** *(transportation);* **WORD ALERT** exception **sion** = *zhun (conclusion)* • one letter combination that makes the *k* sound: **ch** *(anchor)* • one letter combination that makes the *ch* sound: **tu** *(statue)*
Chapter 14: **Silent Letters**	Presents ten silent letters (or combinations): **k** *(knife);* **w** *(wrench);* **b** *(comb);* **gh** *(light);* **h** *(hour);* **g** *(sign);* **s** *(island);* **t** *(whistle);* **l** *(palm);* **p** *(receipt)*
Chapter 15: **Contractions and Word Endings with Long-Vowel Roots**	Summarizes: • contractions • endings **ing, ed, er** • pronunciation of **ed** past tense *(īd, t, d)*
Appendices	Summarize and present examples of information and skills learned throughout Book Three.
Appendix A: **Names**	Presents examples of proper names (male, female, first, last) for every letter of the English alphabet using long vowels and special sounds
Appendix B: **Proverbs**	Summarizes the fifteen proverbs taught on the *Bonus* Pages Highlights the phonetic elements the proverbs emphasize, noting the chapters in which they appear
Appendix C: **Geography**	Presents the names of major geographical areas using long vowels and special sounds: continents, countries, cities, and the fifty states of the United States

Appendix D:
Homonyms

Summarizes some common homonyms using long vowels and special sounds

Appendix E:
Foreign Words in Common English Usage

Introduces foreign words that are used commonly in English but follow different phonetic rules

Appendix F:
Major Sounds of the Consonants and Vowels

Summarizes the variety of major sounds that each letter or combination of letters makes

Stories

Book Three contains seven stories. They illustrate the specific phonetic elements taught in preceding chapters and review some phonetic elements from earlier chapters. The themes of the stories center on adult concerns (work and relationships with family, friends, and colleagues) within the limits of the vocabulary and the phonetic elements students have learned.

If students have mastered the pages preceding the stories, they will be able to read them with ease. In fact, they will be amazed at the high level of complexity and achievement they have reached, even early in the book. The stories provide a great reward for learning.

How to Use the Major Teaching Devices

Three major teaching devices (the *Read, Write,* and *Listen and write* sections) appear throughout the book and are the foundation of the *Essentials of Reading and Writing English* program.

Read

How to Use the *Read* Section

The mechanism of the *Read* section is basically the same for *Sounds, Words, Sentences,* and *Stories.*

As emphasized in Books One and Two, concentrate on the sound of the letter. When reading an individual sound, say the sound the letter makes, not the name of the letter. For example, on page 42 of the student text, where the lesson is **ai** sounds like **a**, read **ai** as *ā*, and encourage each reader to say *ā, ā, ā,* not **A** *(ay)*, **I** *(eye)*, **A, I, A, I.** Start by reading the target sound, then build the words on the sound.

Explain to students that they are going to read the sound *ā*. Point to **ai** at the top of the page and tell them that **ai** sounds like *ā*, and point to **a.** Then say it sounds like **ai** in the word *rain.* (Point to the illustration of rain at the top right corner of the page.)

Students read **ai** *(ā)*, **ai, ai . . .** across the top *Read* line. Then they write **ai** on the *Write* line. When they are ready, you dictate *ā* and they write **ai** on the *Listen and write* line.

Consider using the following successful reading strategies:

1. *Teacher reads first.* Read some examples to students. Ask them to listen and repeat what you read. For example, say:

Listen to the (sounds/words/sentences) I read. Listen especially for the (new/vowel) sounds. Look at the (sounds/words/ sentences) while I read them. Then read after me.

> **Note**
> *Advantage of Listen and repeat method:* At the beginning, students can match sounds with letters.
> *Possible disadvantage:* Students may chant and chorus by rote what they have just heard rather than read it.

2. *Students read first.* The teacher then repeats, correcting their pronunciation. (Do individual reading, which is preferable; have group reading, if necessary.)

   Use either or both of the following strategies:

   a. Chain reading. Have students read around the room. Indicate the order you want, having each student read one sound, word, or sentence in turn.

   b. Random order reading. If students' attention wanders, do not preassign order. Call on them in random order. Not knowing when they will be called on will encourage them to follow along as the reading progresses.

Write

How to Use the *Write* Section

The mechanism of the *Write* section is basically the same for *Sounds, Words, Sentences,* and *Stories.*

1. Have students *Write* only after reading. Decide if they should write after each item or at the end of the *Read* section. (It is preferable to write immediately after each item, since this reinforces both the reading and the writing.)

> **Note**
> Throughout the lesson, make sure that students' pronunciation is correct (or at least being attempted). Also check to ensure that they understand that particular letters represent particular sounds.

2. Allow students to use either hand printing or script.

> **Note**
> Encourage the use of script, since it is the most common form of written communication, especially for adults. Do not, however, discourage printing if it enables the reading to progress more smoothly. You and the students can always return to any point in the text to practice writing a passage in script. The object of the *Write* section is dual—to reinforce the reading and to write.

3. Have students copy the words, not write them from memory. Encourage them to look at the printed letters in the text before they write. This technique helps reinforce the similarities and differences between book type, hand printing, and script. (Students will write from memory in the *Listen and write* section.)

4. Encourage students to say each sound quietly to themselves as they write it.

5. Walk among the group to provide assistance, immediate correction, reassurance, and support.

Listen and write

How to Use the *Listen and write* Section

The mechanism of the *Listen and write* section is basically the same for *Sounds, Words, Sentences,* and *Stories.*

Listen and write is a critical part of the lesson. It forces students to focus their attention. It also indicates to them and to you whether or not they know the sound, word, or sentence. Students may think they hear the difference between the sounds, but it is only in *Listen and write* that they will see what they do and do not understand.

Although this section can be used as a test, its main objective is to clarify students' concepts of the sound before they progress to the next step—a slightly more advanced level.

Listen and write can be rewarding for many students, but very difficult for others. It is not necessary to complete all the *Listen and write* lines. Sometimes doing just a few will make the point. Sometimes all are needed as a review before advancing. Use your discretion in using this teaching tool to evaluate your students' progress.

As you begin *Listen and write:*

1. Tell students to use a piece of paper to cover the part of the page you will be dictating.

2. Dictate any or all of the sounds, words, sentences, or parts of sentences in the *Read* line, either in the order given or in random order.

3. Mark the order of the items you use in your own book.

When students have finished, have volunteers write the list on the board. Correct and compliment their attempts. Indicate that you know how difficult this work is, but explain that it will improve students' vocabulary, spelling, and listening skills. Then repeat the exercise, if desired, with a few more items. Any unused space on the paper can be used by students to practice writing the words they missed.

You might find it helpful at first to dictate only two or three items, stop and correct them, then proceed with another two or three. Don't overwhelm students. Never introduce a feeling of failure.

How to Use the Major Text Sections

Like the other books in this series, *Essentials of Reading and Writing English* Book Three makes use of the *Read, Write,* and *Listen and write* approach to learning. (See pages 117–119 of this manual for details.) These activities occur within the context of a patterned presentation of material. The sections described below appear throughout the book and should be handled the same way each time they appear. Read the general strategies for using each section described here, then refer to the specific chapter discussions for additions and variations to these strategies.

Sound and Sentences   Each sound is presented on two pages: A *Sound* page and a *Sentences* page. The target sound appears alone, in words, and in words in sentences. The sounds, words, and sentences follow the basic, consistent methodology of *Read, Write,* and *Listen and write*.

Sound

How the Use the *Sound* Page

As the first page of each sound, it presents:

1. Sound: *Read, Write, Listen and write*

Once students have learned to *Read* the sound, they can *Write* it; once they can *Write* the sound, they can *Listen and write* it. Remind them that they are listening to the same sound they have just written.

2. Compare: Contrast the target sound to other related but different sounds or similar sounds with different spellings: *Read, Write, Listen and write*

3. Words: A list of ten simple words to *Read, Write, Listen and write*

Once students can read and write a sound, they can read and write simple words containing that sound because they know the surrounding letters. Once they can read simple words, they can read multisyllabic words and sentences.

Compare

The objective of the *Compare* section is to compare the new sound and spelling to sounds and spellings already learned that are similar to or different from the new one.

For example, see **ay** = *ā* on page 44 of the student text. Say:

This is the new sound **ay** *(ā)*. It sounds like **ā.** Here it is in the word *hay* (point to the word and the picture at the top right of the page, and to *hay* on the *Compare* line). **Ay** sounds like *ā* in *cane* (point to *cane* on the *Compare* line) and to *gate.* Continue pointing to words on the *Compare*

line as you say: But it is different from *ă* in *at*. Here it sounds like
ai *(ā)* in *rain*. Now let's read the next line: **ay, and** (ask: *Is* and *the*
same? No.) **ay, act** (*Is* act *the same?* No.) **ay, average** (*Is either* **a** *in*
average *the same?* No.) **ay, ant** (*Is* ant *the same?* No.) **ay, day** (*Is* day *the*
same? Yes.)

After students *Read* and *Write* the sounds, dictate the *Listen and write* to them
from the *Compare* lines.

Sentences   ## How to Use the *Sentences* Page

As the second page for each target sound, it presents additional words in a box and
a **WORD ALERT** section (see pages 120–121 of this manual). The additional words
in the box are arranged in the order that would be most helpful to students—
sometimes alphabetically, other times by the sound of the endings, beginning with
the simplest words and endings, then blends, then multisyllabic words by number
of syllables.

Sentences (usually six, but at least six lines of print) each contain several words
with the target sound. The emphasis in these *Sound* and *Sentences* pages is on
building up and reinforcing already mastered skills.

Encourage students not to be afraid of the multisyllabic words in the box. Show
them that the larger words are made up of smaller parts, each of which they can
read. They have had experience in Book Two with multisyllabic words; if they
have mastered each step along the way, they can progress with confidence to the
next with assured success.

Read the additional words with the class. You might read some sample words
first, then let them read the words. If you think it is appropriate and not overwhelming for your students, have them *Write* and/or *Listen and write* some or all
of the words. For extra practice, you may want to suggest that students write (or
print) at home the words that they can already read.

For example, see page 45 in the student text. Say:

The sound is *ā.* Read down the first column, and listen to the *ā*
sound as you read: *bay, Fay, gay, lay, May,* etc. Point out that
some words have blends, but are still built around the *ā* sound: clay, play, *etc.*
Call attention to two- and three-syllable words: *mid—way, be—tray—er, pay—*
mas—ter.

Sentences

Have students take turns reading one sentence at a time. Repeat it to clarify pronunciation. Ask questions to be sure that students understand the meaning. Explain
new vocabulary if necessary. When it is clear that the class understands the sentence,
read it again, then have students read it as a group.

Note
Emphasize the target sound. As an optional activity, have students underline the key
sound in the sentences, either in the *Read* section before they write, or in their own
handwriting after they have written.

Have students *Write* the sentences (either following each sentence or after all the
sentences have been read). For *Listen and write*, dictate whole sentences or parts
of sentences, depending on the interest and ability of your students.

Word Alert

How to Use the *WORD ALERT* Sections

The *WORD ALERT* sections contain words that are exceptions to the sound being taught; for example, words that are similar in spelling but have different sounds (e.g., page 20: **age** in *average* sounds like *ĭj,* not **age**). When the *WORD ALERT* section is large enough to merit an entire page, rather than a subdivision of the word box on the *Sentences* page, it is followed by *Read, Write,* and *Listen and write.*

Emphasize the part of the word that differs. Students can *Read, Write,* or *Listen and write* some or all, even if it is just a small section of the word box.

Review Pages

How to Use the *Review* Pages

Review pages appear at the end of each chapter. They bring together all the phonetic elements taught in the chapter, including related *WORD ALERT* sections. They also summarize the similarities and differences between the various sounds in the chapter. Sentences using words with the phonetic elements demonstrate how they sound in context and how they are used, and provide an opportunity to compare and contrast them.

Read sounds and words: Read across the page, from left to right.

Read sentences: Look for different sounds in each sentence. Students can underline the sound(s) that you specify.

Write: When students are ready to write the sentences, encourage them to say each one aloud quietly to themselves before they write.

Listen and write: Before you dictate the sentences, tell students to cover the top part of the page. You can use either fixed order or mixed order. Using mixed order is a valuable way to see if students are comprehending the material, not just memorizing it.

Additional Activities

These pages can be used in many different ways (underlining specific elements, creating new sentences, testing skills, etc.).

Bonus pages

How to Use the *Bonus* Pages—Idioms and Proverbs

The *Bonus* pages offer a special feature to enhance teaching and learning. Idioms and proverbs with specific phonetic elements are introduced at the end of relevant chapters.

Proverbs are presented without explanation, since their form rarely changes. Each *Idiom,* however, is presented with a definition and an example sentence that shows how to use it in context.

Explain that idioms are a figurative and descriptive way of speaking, not literal. Add that these expressions are commonly used.

Although the *Bonus* pages are not required, they can be enriching fun, since they provide insight into the expressions used daily by many people in the U.S.

Note

Bonus pages with idioms and/or proverbs appear at the ends of the following chapters: Chapter 3, page 39; Chapter 4, page 57; Chapter 5, page 82; Chapter 6, page 93; Chapter 7, page 109; Chapter 9, page 131; Chapter 10, pages 150–151; Chapter 11, pages 177, 178–179; Chapter 12, page 199; Chapter 13, page 213; Chapter 14, page 226.

Stories

How to Use the *Stories*

Objectives

- To use the phonetic elements and sight words learned so far in a meaningful context

- To give students a sense of accomplishment

Emphasize to students that they can read these stories because they have already learned the phonetic elements from which they are built.

Phonetic Specifications

Each story is followed by a chart of the sounds that are emphasized in the story. The chart also lists sounds from previous stories. Tell students that the current story emphasizes these sounds that they already know. You might read the list of sounds if you think it would be helpful.

Themes

The stories expose students to a wide scope of topics and technical information. The main characters, drawn from a cross section of the ethnic richness in the United States, serve as role models with which students can identify.

The stories in Book Three cover the following themes:

Story 1: Paco and Rosa Santiago, Medical Students (pages 15–16)
   Theme: A young Hispanic-American married couple, medical students with social consciences and strong commitments, do more than their share to help people all over the world.

Story 2: Stevenson's Bakery (pages 36–38)
   Theme: A middle-aged working-class married couple strive together to build up their bakery business.

Stories 3, 4, and 5: A Refugee's Odyssey (pages 79–81, 106–108, 146–149)
   Theme: A Southeast-Asian immigrant family is followed through three stages of their lives, ranging from their escape from their war-torn country (*Story 3: The Escape*), to their adaptation to life in the United States (*Story 4: The Adjustment*), to financial and social success (*Story 5: Real Estate*).

Story 6: Auto Maintenance (pages 209–212)
   Theme: Two men—one black, one white—business partners and friends work hard and succeed. A successful black businesswoman is also featured.

Story 7: Patricia Knowlton's Job-Hunting Campaign (pages 233–237)
   Theme: A white single mother of two develops job-hunting skills and strategies.

Vocabulary

The vocabulary taught in the stories emphasizes the phonetic content of the lessons and offers students growing expertise and awareness of the terminology in these areas as well as insight into cooperative relationships:

Story 1: medicine and geography

Story 2: baking and catering

Story 3: escape and survival

Story 4: American landscape, household, occupations

Story 5: real estate

Story 6: auto maintenance

Story 7: computer field, job-hunting skills, sample résumé, covering letter, help-wanted ads

Previewing Key Words

The stories contain many multisyllabic words, which are introduced in the pages preceding each story. (These pages are entitled "Previewing Key Words of Three or More Syllables from . . .") The words are presented in the order in which they appear in the story, and appear both as whole words and divided into syllables. Repetitions from previous stories appear in the TM section for the page, entitled "Additional Key Words." (Standard for syllabication and definitions: *Webster's Ninth New Collegiate Dictionary,* Merriam-Webster, 1986.) When there is a disparity between the number of syllables in the common pronunciation and the dictionary syllabication, the common pronunciation is presented. (See student book page 14 for more information.)

Read the example word(s) in syllables for students and have them repeat. Then read the whole word, with students chorusing. For example, see page 13. Read **San—ti—a—go; Santiago.** Have individuals continue reading the list, one word (in syllables and whole) at a time, as you repeat to clarify pronunciation, and the class repeats in chorus. Encourage the class to look at the words and read them as they chorus, not just repeat them by ear, which is the temptation. (However, even if students repeat by ear, such repetition is better than nothing, since it reinforces pronunciation. The chain reading guarantees each student a chance to read aloud.)

For *Listen and write,* dictate whole words only.

After students have read the *Previewing* pages, they will be prepared to read everything in the stories. These multisyllabic words have the specific sounds taught in this and previous chapters, and they contain nothing that students have not already learned. If the readability level appears high, it is still quite masterable. The high readability is an advantage that can be effectively dealt with, as long as the material is presented in the context of merely linking sounds and syllables already learned.

Instructional Sequence for the *Stories*

1. *Read aloud in class:* Students may prepare ahead of class by reading silently or aloud to themselves at home, but this is not required. Read around the room, chain reading. Indicate the order you want to use, having each student read one sentence. If students' attention wanders, call on them in random order. Not knowing when they will be called on will encourage them to follow along as the reading progresses.

2. *Call attention to the subheadings:* Explain that each subhead tells the theme of the paragraph that follows. Encourage students to use subheads as clues to the subject. (For example, see student text pages 15 and 16, subheads **On the Job, Do They Relax?, On the Go.**)

3. *Ask questions to ensure comprehension:* Discussion questions for each story are suggested in this Teacher's Manual. The questions are numbered to correspond to the paragraphs in the story, so that you can help students find the answers easily. In addition, try to relate the stories to the lives of your students by asking such questions as *Have you ever done this? Do you know anyone who has? How did you feel? What would you recommend?*

Note

The stories are adult-oriented and contain valuable work-related vocabulary. They become progressively more complex phonetically, but even at a simple level in the early stories, there is a surprisingly large amount of technical vocabulary presented.

---

4. *Phonetic specifications box:* At the end of each story is a box listing the phonetic elements that the story emphasizes from that chapter and reviews from previous chapters. It may be helpful to read this box with your class before reading the story. You can say: *This story emphasizes these sounds that you just learned: . . . It also includes sounds that you learned before, such as . . . .*

5. *Optional skill reinforcement:* Have students underline words in the story that include specific sounds with which you think they need help. They may do this underlining before or after they read. Sometimes it is helpful to have them do this before the reading to reinforce the idea that they know the sounds in these passages (if they seem overwhelmed). But do not make it tedious; sometimes underlining one paragraph is enough. Overall, reading the stories should be fun, not complicated with burdensome extra tasks.

6. *Optional class activities:*

   a. Use the stories as plays. Have students take roles and act out the parts. They can read from the text, memorize the dialogue, or invent their own lines.

   b. If possible, bring in items mentioned in the stories, for example, a baker's tube (Story 2). You might also want to draw some items on the board, such as a cone, a cube, a scalene triangle.

   c. Artistically inclined students may want to draw their interpretations of a particular story.

7. *Optional field trips:* Visit places like the ones identified in the stories. Possible field trips for each story include the following: *Story 1:* a local teaching hospital, a travel agency; *Story 2:* a bakery, a vocational school; *Story 4:* U.S. immigration office, U.S. countryside, city, coast; *Story 5:* a real estate office; *Story 6:* an auto repair shop; *Story 7:* a computer company, the local state employment division (the latter may provide application forms that students can practice filling out).

Unit One: Long Vowels

This unit has two main emphases:

1. Review of the short vowels and the concept of multisyllabic words.

2. Introduction of long vowels in open syllables and with silent **e.**

The review and introduction chapters in this unit follow the same basic methodology used in Books One and Two: *Read, Write,* and *Listen and write.* (Refer to "How to Use the Major Teaching Devices" on pages 117–124 of this manual.)

The silent **e** sections in this unit have a particular format: essentially two pages plus additional pages for the *WORD ALERT* section as needed. See, for example, pages 18–20: *Long-Vowel ā with Silent* **e.**

The first page (page 18) begins with a comparison between short vowels and long vowels with silent **e,** all in the *Read, Write,* and *Listen and write* format. The emphasis here is that by just adding a silent **e** you can change the whole sound of the word, making a different word with a different meaning. This is followed by a list of twenty-four simple words with long vowels and silent **e** (generally one syllable, with few blends, usually arranged by ending sounds) for *Read, Write,* and *Listen and write.*

The second page (page 19) contains a list of additional words with the same long vowels and silent **e** (some multisyllabic, with blends and special sounds previously learned in Books One and Two). Following these are sentences, usually six or at least six lines of print, containing those words and emphasizing that sound to *Read, Write,* and *Listen and write.*

The third page (page 20) lists words that are exceptions to the sound being taught, but close enough to be included in the lesson. (See "How to Use the *Word Alert* Sections" on page 121 of this manual.)

Chapter 1: Introduction to Long Vowels

Page 2 English Class Bulletin

Point out that the Bulletin is written in newspaper style. Its purpose is to welcome the class to Book Three. (See Book Two, pages 226–227, Story 12: *The Crystal Junction Banner.*)

Pages 3–4 Review: Short-Vowel Words with Two or More Syllables and Special Sounds

Ask the class for additional items for review section (for example, *family, Benjamin, competition*). Chain read around the room.

Page 5 Introduction to Long Vowels

To help acclimate students to the difference between short and long vowels, copy the chart from section C on the board:

	Short Vowels		Long Vowels
ă	apple	ā	ape
ĕ	egg	ē	he
ĭ	inch	ī	ice
ŏ	olive	ō	no
ŭ	umbrella	ū	cubic
y̆	gym	ȳ	sky

Point to the appropriate column as you read the items to the class.

Chapter 2: Long Vowels with Open Syllables

Page 6   **A. Comparing Closed and Open Syllables**

When you are sure that students understand sentences 1 and 2 in section A, point to *hen* in the first column and ask:

Why is this a *closed* syllable? (It ends with a consonant.) Which letter is the vowel? (e) How does the vowel sound? (ĕ as in *egg*) Is it the long or the short sound? (short) How can you tell? (the short-vowel mark ˘)

Then point to *he* in the second column and ask:

Why is this an *open* syllable? (It doesn't end with a consonant.) Which letter is the vowel? (e) How does the vowel sound? (ē as in *feet*) Is it the long or the short sound? (long) How can you tell? (the long-vowel mark ¯) Does the vowel say its name? (Yes, except for **y,** which says ī like *I*.)

You may want to repeat with open and closed syllables for each of the remaining vowels, encouraging students to say the long sounds.

> **Note**
> Check frequently during this lesson to be sure that students understand the difference between the short-vowel mark [˘] and the long-vowel mark [¯].

Page 7   **B. Long Vowels with Open Syllables at the End of Words**

Explain that these new words are based on the same idea of open syllables, with the long vowel at the end of the word.

Point out that the final vowel in each word is in boldface type. Ask students to tell you how each final vowel sounds (vowel's name, except for **y** = ī).

C. Long Vowels with Open Syllables Inside of Words

Explain that these new words have the long vowels inside them, but at the end of a syllable. Point out that the following consonant begins the next syllable.

Ask students to find the open syllable inside each word, pointing out the boldfaced letters. After each one has been identified, ask:

Why is it open? (vowel has long sound; no consonant at the end of the syllable; the following consonant begins the next syllable)

You may want to demonstrate on the board; for example, the word *lady*:

1. **a** has the long-vowel sound

2. no consonant at the end of the first syllable *(la)*

3. consonant **d** begins next syllable

Page 8   Two-Syllable, Long-Vowel Words

This page offers two-syllable words with open syllables and first-syllable long vowels. Have students underline the long vowel in each word.

Read each word in syllables, then as a whole word, and have students repeat. They should then write each word twice in the space provided, the first time in syllables if you think they need practice with the concept.

Pages 9–10   Words with Long-Vowel Prefixes

Explain that these two- and three-syllable words have open syllables called prefixes. Tell students that a prefix is a syllable (or syllables) that comes at the beginning of a word and changes its meaning in some way.

Read each word in syllables, then as a whole word, and have students repeat. They should then write each word twice in the space provided.

Page 11   Contractions Using Long Vowels

Point out that the long vowels are inside each contraction. Be sure that students understand that each contraction is a shortened form of the two words in the first column. (Remind students that they learned many of these contractions in Book Two.)

Write: Have students write the words *and* the contractions, or the contractions only (twice).

Page 12   Review: Long Vowels in Open Syllables

Explain the idiom *to fly off the handle* as "to lose control."

Pages 13–14   Special Skill: Previewing Key Words of Three or More Syllables from Story 1

NOTE: See pages 130 of this manual for pronunciation of words with *ire*.

Additional Words from Story 1

Remind students that they have already learned most of these additional words. If possible, provide paper so that they can practice sounding out and writing the words. Ask volunteers to list them on the board.

1. prac ti cal	practical		7. ex am ple	example
2. ad di tion	addition		8. un der stand	understand
3. hos pi tal	hospital		9. tal ent ed	talented
4. at ten tion	attention		10. vis it ed	visited
5. ad dict ed	addicted		11. con struct ed	constructed
6. com mit ting	committing			

Additional Activities

1. Ask students to list the words in alphabetical order by first letter only. (Group all the "a" words, all the "b" words, and so on.) For more challenge, have them list them in alphabetical order through the second letter.

2. If you have dictionaries available, encourage students to look up each word and write its definition beside it. (You may want to do two or three at a time.)

3. More advanced students may want to try using the words in sentences.

Pages 15–16

Story 1: Paco and Rosa Santiago, Medical Students

This story consolidates the skills taught in Chapters 1 and 2. (See "How to Use the *Stories*" on pages 122–124 of this manual and the phonetic specifications following the story in the text.)

Discussion Questions

Select from the following questions those that are appropriate for your class; ask other questions as well. Encourage students to respond, to give their answers and opinions, and to ask additional questions. This will help them comprehend the information in the story and gain confidence in their growing abilities.

Paragraph 1: Where did Paco and Rosa meet? *(on campus, at a college in Ohio)* What were they doing there? *(premedical students)* (NOTE: Explain that *status quo* is a Latin phrase that means "the way things are now.")

Paragraph 2: What two major things do Rosa and Paco do? *(study; assist at the local hospital for training with no pay)* (NOTE: You may want to introduce the word *volunteer,* "to choose to do something for no pay." [**ee** *(ē)* will be taught in Chapter 5])

Students might want to know what it means to *observe* eight specific tasks. Help them understand that *observe* means "to watch and listen."

1. *prenatal* = before birth, during pregnancy; 2. *investigations* = research (**ear** will be taught in Chapter 11); 3. *prolapsed uterus* = organ where fetus is nurtured slipped out of place (if you have chart of the human body, you may want to point to the uterus); 4. *afebrile* = not having a fever (temperature not above 98.6° F); 5. *acne* = noncatching skin disease, often causing pimples (sometimes controlled with medication); 6. point out that prescriptions are filled in a pharmacy (**ar** will be taught in Chapter 11; **ph** in Chapter 12); 7. *ether* = an anesthetic that is used in operations; 8. drug and alcohol *abuse* (**u** will be taught in Chapter 8)

Paragraph 3: (Explain: *asocial* = not social, exhibiting hostile behavior)

Paragraph 4: (Explain: *to get dry* = to stop drinking alcohol) What is a precinct? *(local police station)*

Paragraph 5: (Explain: *secret cult* = group of people meeting in secret, devoted to a leader or belief generally regarded as unusual)

Paragraph 6: (Explain: *pump iron* = lift weights) What do Rosa and Paco do for relaxation? *(bicycle; pushups; pump iron; watch TV)*

Paragraphs 7–8: How do Paco and Rosa get to travel? *(as volunteer medical helpers)* How are their trips paid for? *(hospital patrons donate the money)* Where have Paco and Rosa gone? *(Iceland, China, Cuba, Tokyo)*

Paragraph 9: What do Paco and Rosa do for themselves? What do they do for others? How do they feel about the environment? *(See text.)* What kind of people are they? *(super, vital human beings)*

Chapter 3: Long Vowels with Silent e

Page 17   One effective way to introduce this concept is to present the information in three columns: one of vowels and two identical columns of short-vowel words:

a	cap	cap
e	let	let
i	kit	kit
o	rob	rob
u	cub	cub

Add the short mark (˘) at the top of the first column of words, and point out that the vowel has the short sound in the words in that column. Then explain that you will make the second column of words have the long-vowel sound by adding a silent **e** to the end. Ask students to tell you what the silent **e** means. It doesn't "say" anything but it makes the vowel before it long (say its name). Tell them that the silent **e** has the power to change the vowel before it from the short sound to a long one.

Put the long mark (¯) at the top of the second column of words, then add an **e** to the end of *cap*. Point to it and point out that the word is now *cape*. Have students pronounce it after you say it. Complete each word in the third column, then draw an arrow from the silent **e** to the vowel:

cape   athlete   kite   robe   cube

Read across the chart, comparing the short and long vowels: cap, cape; let, athlete; kit, kite; rob, robe; cub, cube. Ask:

Do you hear the short vowel? Do you hear the long vowel?

When students are ready, have them write the short- and long-vowel words in the appropriate columns. Make sure they notice the short and long marks before they begin to write.

Read sentences: Call attention to the use of short- and long-vowel words in each sentence. Ask:

Does *cap* have a short- or long-vowel **a**? *(short)* Does *athlete* have a short- or long-vowel **e**? *(long)* Does *kite* have a short- or long-vowel **i**? *(long)* Does *rob* have a short- or a long-vowel **o**? *(short)* Does *cube* have a short- or long-vowel **u**? *(long)*

Pages 18–19   Long Vowel *ā* with Silent e

This two-page lesson is the model for the vowels with silent **e** taught in this chapter. The same basic format is used to teach all the long vowels—**a, e, i, o, u** (**y** is combined with **i**).

Page 18   Introduce the long vowel with silent **e.** Call attention to the word and the picture at the top right of the student text page, pointing out the **a–e** in *cape*.

Read and compare the four short- and long-vowel words, then have students write them in the space provided.

Listen and write: Dictate the eight words presented in mixed order.

Read and *Write:* Have students read the words listed. Call attention to the words grouped by endings: **ace, ade, age, ake, ale, ame, ane, ape, ase, ate, ave, aze.** Have students write the words in the spaces provided. Encourage them to say each word aloud quietly as they write.

Listen and write: Dictate one word from each group.

Page 19   Read the words in the box with students. (NOTE: Words are grouped in various ways: by endings—**fade, jade, blade, evade;** alphabetically; and in compound-word groups with similar roots—*baseball, football, basketball,* see page 185.)

Additional Activities

1. Have students underline the long vowel, the consonant, and the silent **e** in each **a–e** word in the sentences.

2. Have students select one or two columns from the box to alphabetize.

Page 20   ## *WORD ALERT*

Explain that sometimes **a** with silent **e** sounds like ĭ in *it*. Complete the section, following the suggestions on page 121 of this manual.

Page 23   ## Long-Vowel ī with Silent e

Explain that the **ire** ending is frequently pronounced like two syllables *(i—er)*, even though the dictionary treats **ire** as a one-syllable sound and doesn't divide it for spelling purposes. Emphasize also that **re** as an ending sounds like **er,** not **re.**

Dictionary	Pronunciation
fire	fi · er
wire	wi · er
de · sire	de · si · er
en · tire	en · ti · er
tire · less	ti · er · less
re · tire	re · ti · er
re · quired	re · qui · er(e)d (NOTE: Third **e** is silent.)

Page 32   ## *WORD ALERT:* Sometimes u with Silent e Makes New Sounds

See Chapter 13 on pages 152–153 of this manual for development of the **tu** = *ch* and **su** = *sh* sounds.

Pages 34–35   ## Special Skill: Previewing Key Words of Three or More Syllables from Story 2

(NOTE: See page 130 of this manual for pronunciation of words with **ire.**)

Additional Words from Story 2

Remind students that they have already learned most of these additional words. If possible, provide paper so that they can practice sounding out and writing the words. Ask volunteers to list them on the board.

NOTE: Explain that the word *business* is pronounced in two syllables: **biz—ness**. Point out that it is different from the three-syllable word *positive (pos—i—tive)*, where **i** is a separate syllable.

1. ba na na   banana
2. cran ber ry   cranberry
3. ex cel lent   excellent
4. el e gant   elegant
5. dif fi cult   difficult
6. what ev er   whatever

Pages 36–38   ## Story 2: Stevenson's Bakery

This story consolidates the skills taught in Chapters 1 through 3. (See "How to Use the *Stories*" on pages 122–124 of this manual and the phonetic specifications following the story in the text.)

Discussion Questions

Select from the following questions those that are appropriate for your class; ask other questions as well. Encourage students to respond, to give their answers and opinions, and to ask additional questions. This will help them comprehend the information in the story and gain confidence in their growing abilities.

Paragraph 1: Describe Mike and Grace Stevenson. *(middle-aged, husband and wife, bakers)*

Paragraph 2: What types of cakes do they bake? *(many, including chocolate, white, yellow, spice, banana; some with nuts)* Are they all made with sugar? *(no; some are sugarless and nonfattening)* What kinds of people want these cakes? *(people on restricted diets, those who are diabetic or allergic, those concerned with nutrition)*

Paragraph 3: For what occasions do Mike and Grace make cakes? *(Mike likes to make wedding cakes; Grace makes cakes for any occasion; miniature cakes for private, intimate evenings, huge cakes for celebrations)*

Paragraph 4: Name the shapes of the cakes they make. *(basic cake shapes; cubes, cones, domes, scalene triangles)* (NOTE: Draw the shapes on the board, or pass around a dictionary that illustrates these geometric figures.)

Paragraph 5: What kinds of cakes do Grace and Mike make for children? for athletes? *(kites, planes, animals for children; bikes and ice skates for athletes)*

Paragraph 6: Describe the cake decorations. *(See text.)*

Paragraph 7: (Explain: *mate* = groom [taught in Chapter 9]; *elope* = couple runs away to get married)

Paragraph 8: (Explain: *chrome* = shiny silver-colored metal)

Paragraph 9: What does Grace prefer to do? *(bake)* What kind of musical themes does she duplicate when she decorates? *(flute, tuba, trombone, notes on a staff)* (NOTE: If possible, show pictures of the musical instruments.)

Paragraph 10: (Explain: *replicate* = copy; *innovative* = doing things in new, creative ways; *infinite* = endless, having no limit)

Paragraph 11: Do Mike and Grace try to please their customers? *(yes)*

Paragraph 12: What kind of delivery service do they provide? *(within 25 miles; on-time)*

Paragraph 13: What catering services do they offer? *(competitive prices; elegant cakes on nice plates; tables with lace tablecloths)*

Paragraph 14: What is Stevenson's Cafe? *(patio at the side of the bakery)* What does *cafe* mean? *(a place to buy and eat small meals, from french* café *= coffee)*

Paragraph 15: What does the cafe look like? *(patio paved in flagstone and concrete; shaded by umbrellas and foliage; very nice place)* What is a patio? *(a paved outdoor recreation area next to a building, a place to serve outdoor meals)* What can customers buy to eat on the patio? *(a slice of cake, a beverage)* Do the Stevensons serve full-course meals in the cafe? *(no)*

Paragraph 16: (Explain: *renovate* = change, improve, modernize; *strike while the iron is hot* [see page 39])

Paragraph 17: (Explain: *centigrade* = a scale for measuring temperature; $0°$ C marks the freezing point of water and $100°$ C marks the boiling point. You may want to point out that in the U.S. Fahrenheit is commonly used: $32°$ F = freezing, $212°$ F = boiling; *bite the bullet* [see page 39])

Paragraph 18: (Explain: *apprentice* = someone learning a trade by practical experience; *lecture* = a planned talk on a special subject; *vocational school* = business, professional, or trade school)

Paragraph 19: (Explain *constructive* = useful, helpful)

Unit Two: Long-Vowel Sounds Made from Other Letter Combinations

Explain that until now students have read long-vowel sounds made in two main ways: open syllables *(a pron)*; long-vowels with silent **e** *(cape, athlete, kite, robe, cube)*.

In this unit, they will learn to read other combinations of letters that make the long-vowel sounds. Some combinations resemble the sound (**ai** = *ā,* as in *rain*); others do not look like the sound (**ey** = *ā,* as in *they*). Reassure students that this book will help them learn the many combinations that make the sounds *ā, ē, ī, ō, ū,* by concentrating on each one, one at a time.

> **Note**
> Chapters 4 through 8 offer one chapter for each vowel sound. There are approximately twenty-four combinations, plus ***WORD ALERT*** sections featuring variations—words that are similar and different. Follow the suggestions in "How to Use the Major Teaching Devices" and "How to Use the Major Text Sections" on pages 164–179 of this manual. Variations are noted below.

Chapter 4: The *ā* Sound

Tell students that in this chapter they will learn seven letter combinations that make the *ā* sound (as in *ape* and *cape*), one combination at a time.

Page 42   ### Sound ai = *ā (rain)*

Explain that the **ai** in *rain* sounds like the **a** in *race*. Say *rain* and point to it in the first line of the *Compare* section. Point to *race*. (See suggestions for using the *Compare* section on pages 119–120 of this manual.)

Page 43   ### Sentences with the ai = *ā* Sound

Call attention to the ***WORD ALERT*** section of the box. Emphasize the differences between the words that follow the **ai** = *ā* sound and spelling and those in the ***WORD ALERT***. Encourage students to look for the ***WORD ALERT*** exceptions in the sentences.

Additional Activities

1. Have students underline the featured sound in each sentence.

2. Have students circle the ***WORD ALERT*** exceptions in the sentences.

3. Discuss the differences and similarities between the ***WORD ALERT*** exceptions and the words that follow the featured sound; for example: Is it spelled the same but does it have a different sound? If it has the same sound, is it spelled differently?

Page 44   ## Sound: ay = *ā* (hay)

Explain that the **ay** in *hay* sounds like the *ā* in *rain* and the *ā* in *cane*, etc. Say *hay* and point to it in the first line of the *Compare* section. Then point to *rain*. Then compare with the other words; it is different from *at, and, act, average, ant.*

Page 45   ## Sentences with the ay = *ā* Sound

Call attention to the **WORD ALERT** section. Emphasize the differences between the words that follow the **ay = *ā*** sound and spelling and those in the **WORD ALERT**. Encourage students to find and circle the **WORD ALERT** exceptions in the sentence.

Page 46   ## Sound: ange = *ānj* (danger)

Explain that the **a** in *danger* sounds like the *ā* in *vane* and the *ā* in *day*, etc. Say *danger* and point to it in the first line of the *Compare* section. Compare *danger* with the sounds of the other words; it is different from *anger, bang, tang.*

Page 48   ## Sound: aste = *āst* (paste)

Explain that the **a** in *paste* sounds like the *ā* in *ate* and the *ā* in *hay*, etc. Say *paste* and point to it in the *Compare* section. Compare it with the sounds of the other words; it is different from *as, at.*

Page 49   ## Sentences with the aste = *āst* Sound

Call attention to the **WORD ALERT** section. Emphasize the differences between the words that follow the **aste = *āst*** sound and spelling and the words in the **WORD ALERT**. Encourage students to find and circle the **WORD ALERT** exceptions in the sentences.

Page 50   ## Sound: able = *ābull* (table)

Explain that the **a** in *table* sounds like the *ā* in *Abe*, the *ā* in *may*, etc. Say *table* and point to it in the *Compare* section; it is different from *absent.*

Page 51   ## Sentences with the able = *ābull* Sound

Call attention to the **WORD ALERT** section. Emphasize the differences between the words that follow the **able = *ābull*** sound and spelling and the words in the **WORD ALERT**. Encourage students to find and circle the **WORD ALERT** exceptions in the sentences.

Note

You may want to explain that **able** is also used as a suffix—a combination of letters added to the end of an existing word to make another word. The **WORD ALERT** offers these examples: *change, changeable; check, checkable; comfort, comfortable; recycle, recyclable* (point out the dropped **e**).

Page 52   ## Sound: ey = *ā* (they)

Explain that the **ey** in *they* sounds like the *ā* in *mane*, the *ā* in *manger*, etc. Say *they* and point to it in the *Compare* section; it is different from *let.*

Page 53   ## Sentences with the ey = *ā* Sound

Call attention to the **WORD ALERT** section. Emphasize the differences between the words that follow the **ey = *ā*** sound and spelling and the words in the **WORD ALERT**. Encourage students to find and circle the **WORD ALERT** words in the sentences, then spell out the two words of each contraction they find.

> **Note**
> Call attention to the *Contractions* section. Remind students that a contraction means that two words were shortened into one. Also remind them that they already know some contractions, having learned them combined with other pronouns. At this point, consider using both of these options:
>
> 1. Review the lesson on page 11. Where appropriate, change *you* to *they;*
>
> 2. Move ahead to Chapter 15 and work with students on contractions.

Page 54   ## Sound: ei = *ā (veil)*

Explain that the **ei** in *veil* sounds like the *ā* in *lane*. Say *veil* and point to it in the *Compare* section; it is not different from any of the *Compare* words; it sounds like all the examples of the *ā* sound.

Page 55   ## Sentences with the ei = *ā* Sound

Call attention to the **WORD ALERT** section. Emphasize the differences between the words that follow the **ei = *ā*** sound and spelling and the words in the **WORD ALERT**. Encourage students to find and circle the **WORD ALERT** in the sentences.

> **Note**
> Point out the silent letters **gh**. If you want, teach some of the basics from Chapter 14: **gh** as in *light*.

Chapter 5: The *ē* Sound

Tell students that in this lesson they will learn six letter combinations that make the *ē* sound (as in *he* and *athlete*), one combination at a time.

Page 58   ## Sound: ee = *ē (feet)*

Explain that the **ee** in *feet* sounds like the *ē* in *here* and the *ē* in *Pete*, etc. Say *feet* and point to it in the *Compare* section; it is different from *pest, were, tent, there.*

Page 59   ## Sentences with the ee = *ē* Sound

Call attention to the **WORD ALERT** section. Emphasize the differences between the words that follow the **ee = *ē*** sound and spelling and *been* in the **WORD ALERT**.

Page 60   ## Sound: ea = *ē (leaf)*

Explain that the **ea** in *leaf* sounds like the **ee** in *feet* and the *ē* in *here*, etc. Say *leaf* and point to it in the *Compare* section; it is different from *hen, they.*

Page 61   ## Sentences with the ea = $\bar{e}$ Sound

Discuss with students the many commonly used **ea** = $\bar{e}$ words listed.

Additional Activities

Practice numbers and counting: have students count the number of **ea** = $\bar{e}$ words they find in each sentence. You may want to assign two sentences at a time, or ask students to work in teams of three doing two sentences each. Team figures can then be put on the board and volunteers can total the columns.

Page 63   ## *WORD ALERT:* Sometimes ea = $\breve{e}$ *(bread)*

Although a *WORD ALERT,* this lesson set follows the same format as other *Sound* and *Sentences* pages in the unit because of its many important examples.

Explain that the **ea** in *bread* sounds like the $\breve{e}$ in *egg, get, help,* etc. Say *bread* and point to it in the *Compare* section; it is different from *here, feet, sea, leaf, meet.*

Page 64   ## *WORD ALERT:* Sentences with the ea = $\breve{e}$ Sound

See the discussion for page 61 and "How to Use the *WORD ALERT* Sections" on page 121 of this manual.

Page 65   ## *WORD ALERT:* Sometimes ea Makes Other Sounds

Page 66   ## Sentences with the Other Sounds of ea

These *WORD ALERT* pages have a slightly varied format, although the same principles apply.

Explain that each section notes a different sound of **ea.** Spend as much time on this lesson as necessary; you might want to consider coming back to it for review at a later point in the book.

See the discussion for page 61, and "How to Use the *WORD ALERT* Sections" on page 121 of this manual.

Page 67   ## Sound: ie = $\bar{e}$ *(field)*

Explain that the **ie** in *field* sounds like the **ee** in *feet,* the **ea** in *leaf,* the $\bar{e}$ in *here,* etc. Say *field* and point to it in the *Compare* section; it is different from the second **e** in *even,* and in *bite.*

Page 68   ## Sentences with the ie = $\bar{e}$ Sound

Call attention to the *WORD ALERT* section. Emphasize the differences between the words that follow the **ie** = $\bar{e}$ sound and spelling and the words in the *WORD ALERT* section. Encourage students to find and circle the *WORD ALERT* exceptions in the sentences.

Note

If you want, give students a "preview" of **air** in Chapter 11 and silent **p** in Chapter 14.

Page 69   ## Sound: ei = ē *(ceiling)*

Explain that the **ei** in *ceiling* sounds like the **ee** in *feet*, the **ea** in *leaf*, the *ē* in *athlete*, etc. Say *ceiling* and point to it in the *Compare* section; it is different from *neighbor, they.*

> **Note**
> Call attention to items 1 through 5 in the *Read* column. Discuss with students the spelling rule "**i** before **e** except after **c** or when sounded like **a** as in *neighbor* and *weigh.*" Point out the exceptions to the rule, listed in the *read* column (items 6 through 10). Remind students of this rule and its exceptions as you proceed through the text.

Page 70   ## Sentences with the ei = ē Sound

> **Note**
> Point out the **able** suffix in *conceivable* and *inconceivable,* noting that the silent **e** in *conceive* was dropped before **able** was added.

Call attention to the **WORD ALERT** section. Emphasize the differences between the words that follow the **ei** = *ē* sound and spelling and the words in the **WORD ALERT** section. Encourage students to find and circle the **WORD ALERT** exceptions in the sentences.

Page 71   ## Sound: y = ē *(city)*

Explain that the **y** in *city* sounds like the **ee** in *feet*, the *ē* in *here*, etc. Say *city* and point to it in the *Compare* section; it is different from *gym, my, sky.*

Page 72   ## Sentences with the y = ē Sound

Call attention to the **WORD ALERT** section. Emphasize the differences between the words that follow the **y** = *ē* sound and spelling and the words in the **WORD ALERT** section. Encourage students to find and circle the **WORD ALERT** exceptions in the sentences.

Page 73   ## Sound: i = ē *(ski)*

Explain that the **i** in *ski* sounds like the **ee** in *feet*, the **ea** in *leaf*, etc. Say *ski* and point to it in the *Compare* section; it is different from *pit, pike.*

Page 75   ## *WORD ALERT:* Sometimes i = *yuh* *(petunia)*

Page 76   ## Sentences with the i = *yuh* Sound

Although a **WORD ALERT,** this two-page lesson follows the same format as other *Sound* and *Sentences* pages in the unit because of its many important examples.

Explain that the **i** in *petunia* sounds like the **y** in *yellow.* Say *petunia* and point to it in the *Compare* section; it is different from *pit, bite, ski, gym.*

Page 78   ## Special Skill: Previewing Key Words of Three or More Syllables from Story 3

NOTE: See page 130 of this manual for pronunciation of words with **ire.**

Additional Words from Story 3

Remind students that they have already learned most of these additional words. If possible, provide paper so that they can practice sounding out and writing the words. Ask volunteers to list them on the board.

1. what ev er   whatever

2. beau ti ful   beautiful

3. ev ery thing   everything

Pages 79–81   ## Story 3: A Refugee's Odyssey: Part 1: The Escape

This story consolidates the skills taught in Chapters 4 and 5. (See "How to Use the *Stories*" on pages 122–124 of this manual and the phonetic specifications following the story in the text.)

Discussion Questions

Select from the following questions those that are appropriate for your class; ask other questions as well. Encourage students to respond, to give their answers and opinions, and to ask additional questions. This will help them comprehend the information in the story and gain confidence in their growing abilities.

Paragraph 1: (Explain: *prerevolution* = before the revolution; *ancestors* = those who lived before in the family, previous generations [See Chapter 11: **or**.])

Paragraph 2: Did the family have enough to eat? *(yes)* What did their diet consist of? *(fish, rice, vegetables)*

Paragraph 3: What special event was taking place in the family? *(planning the marriage of young niece to a friend)*

Paragraph 4: (Explain: *revolution* = attack against the established government to bring about change, usually by force) What happened in the village? *(great upheaval; strangers came; people detained in prison; some people shot)*

Paragraph 5: What happened to relationships between people? *(everyone was afraid of neighbors)* What happened to the fields? *(lands were ruined)*

Paragraph 6: How was public health? *(poor; a constant problem)* Who in the family died? Of what? *(Yik Yam's father and baby; of measles)*

Paragraph 7: Did the family decide their future was to stay or flee? *(flee)* How did they get away? *(running, hiding, finally riding in a jeep)*

Paragraph 8: How did they get on a ship? *(bribed the police)*

Paragraph 9: Which members of the family got on the ship? *(Yik Yam, Nari, two children, the niece, the grandmother)* Did they have any possessions? *(no)* Was there enough food on the ship? *(there was very little)* How did they feel on the ship? *(filled with fear)*

Paragraph 10: What happened during the hurricane? *(rain and spray, great winds, huge waves; sails ripped; ship leaked; people heaved freight over the side)*

Paragraph 11: What did the pirates do? *(seized the ship; demanded ransom; seized wealth; kidnapped Yik Yam's niece)*

Paragraph 12: How did the family feel when they arrived at the refugee camp? *(they felt they had reached their limits; ragged, disheveled; depressed)*

Paragraph 13: Which member of the family died in the refugee camp? *(Yik Yam's mother)*

Paragraph 14: What did the family wonder? *(what America was going to be like; what lay ahead)*

Chapter 6: The ī Sound

Tell students that in this lesson they will learn five letter combinations that make the ī sound (as in *ice* and *kite*), one combination at a time.

Page 84   ## Sound: y = ī *(fly)*

Explain that the **y** in *fly* sounds like the ī in *kite*. Say *fly* and point to it in the *Compare* section; it is different from *happy, they, gym, yellow, hay.*

Page 85   ## Sentences with the y = ī Sound

Call attention to the **WORD ALERT** section. Emphasize the differences between the words that follow the **y** = ī sound and spelling and the words in the **WORD ALERT**. Encourage students to find and circle the **WORD ALERT** exceptions in the sentences.

Page 86   ## Sound: ie = ī *(tie)*

Explain that the **ie** in *tie* sounds like the ī in *fine*, the **y** in *sky*, etc. Say *tie* and point to it in the *Compare* section; it is different from *pit, me, field, chief.*

> **Note**
> Call attention to the last three words (items 8 through 10) in the *Read* column, and point out the **ies** and **ied** endings. Explain that in most root words ending in **y** (like *defy, apply, supply*) you change the **y** to **i** when you add **es, ed,** or **er** endings (present or past tense, or comparative adjectives). Tell students they will learn more about this on the *Sentences* page.

Page 87   ## Sentences with the ie = ī Sound

> **Note**
> Be sure that students notice that the box at the top of the page has a format different from the usual box. Point out and define the headings, calling attention to the five forms.

Page 88   ## Sound: igh = ī *(light)*

Explain that the **igh** in *light* sounds like the ī in *kite*, the **ie** in *tie*, etc. Say *light* and point to it in the *Compare* section; it is different from *hog, chief.*

> **Note**
> You may want to have students preview **gh** *(light)* in Chapter 14.

Page 90   Sounds: ild = *īld (child)*; ind = *īnd*
(*find*)

Explain that the **i** in *child* and *find* sounds like the *ī* in *while* and *fine*, etc. Say *child* and *find* and point to them in the *Compare* section; they are different from *chilled*, *finned*.

Page 91   Sentences with the ild = *īld*;
ind = *īnd* Sounds

Call attention to the **WORD ALERT** section. Emphasize the differences between the words that follow the **ild, ind** = *ī* sound and spelling and *wind* (*ĭ*) in the **WORD ALERT**. Then compare and contrast *wĭnd/wīnd;* for example: 1. The storm's *wĭnd* is fierce! 2. Please *wīnd* the string on this spool. Encourage students to look for this **WORD ALERT** in the sentences.

Chapter 7: The *ō* Sound

Tell students that in this lesson they will learn five letter combinations that make the *ō* sound (as in *no* and *robe*), one combination at a time.

Page 94   Sound: oe = *ō (toe)*

Explain that the **oe** in *toe* sounds like the *ō* in *hope*, *go*, etc. Say *toe* and point to it in the *Compare* section; it is different from *hop*.

Page 95   Sentences with the oe = *ō* Sound

Call attention to the **WORD ALERT** section. Emphasize the differences between the words that follow the **oe** = *ō* sound and spelling and the words in the **WORD ALERT**. Encourage students to find and circle the **WORD ALERT** exceptions in the sentences.

Page 96   Sound: oa = *ō (boat)*

Explain that the **oa** in *boat* sounds like the *ō* in *go*, *note*, etc. Say *boat* and point to it in the *Compare* section; it is different from *job*, *hat*, *hate*.

Page 97   Sentences with the oa = *ō* Sound

Call attention to the **WORD ALERT** section. Emphasize the differences between the words that follow the **oa** = *ō* sound and spelling and the words in the **WORD ALERT**. Encourage students to find and circle the **WORD ALERT** exceptions in the sentences.

Page 98   Sound ow = *ō (snow)*

Explain that the **ow** in *snow* sounds like the *ō* in *go*, *note*, etc. Say *snow* and point to it in the *Compare* section; it is different from *mob*, *web*, *son*.

Page 99   Sentences with the ow = *ō* Sound

Call attention to the **WORD ALERT** section. Emphasize the differences between the words that follow the **ow** = *ō* sound and spelling and the words in the **WORD ALERT**.

Page 100   ## Sound: ol = ōl (bolt)

Explain that the **ol** in *bolt* sounds like the *ōl* in *hole, goal,* etc. Say *bolt* and point to it in the *Compare* section; it is different from *nod, lock.*

Page 102   ## Sound: ost = ōst (post)

Explain that **ost** in *post* sounds like the *ō* in *pose,* the **oa** in *boat,* etc. Say *post* and point to it in the *Compare* section; it is different from *sob, son, cost.*

Page 103   ## Sentences with the ost = ōst Sound

Call attention to the **WORD ALERT** section. Point out the silent **h** in *ghost.* Encourage students to look for this **WORD ALERT** in the sentences.

Page 105   ## Special Skill: Previewing Key Words of Three or More Syllables from Story 4

NOTE: See page 130 of this manual for pronunciation of words with **ire**.

Additional Words from Story 4

Remind students that they have already learned most of these additional words. If possible, provide paper so that they can practice sounding out and writing the words. Ask volunteers to list them on the board.

1. re main ing	remaining		14. ev ery day	everyday
2. fin al ly	finally		15. ev ery thing	everything
3. de mand ed	demanded		16. con di tion	condition
4. in clud ing	including		17. ex cel lent	excellent
5. de ter mined	determined		18. cus tom ers	customers
6. o ver come	overcome		19. in de pen dent	independent
7. ref u gee	refugee		20. hes i tant ly	hesitantly
8. od ys sey	odyssey		21. ac cept ed	accepted
9. dif fi cult	difficult		22. pos si ble	possible
10. im pos si ble	impossible		23. what ev er	whatever
11. un der stand	understand		24. in ter est	interest
12. con stant ly	constantly		25. an oth er	another
13. beau ti ful	beautiful		26. dif fer ent	different

Pages 106–108   ## Story 4: A Refugee's Odyssey: Part 2: The Adjustment

This story consolidates the skills taught in Chapters 5, 6, and 7. (See "How to Use the *Stories*" on pages 122–124 of this manual and the phonetic specifications following the story in the text.)

Discussion Questions

Select from the following questions those that are appropriate for your class; ask other questions as well. Encourage students to respond, to give their answers and opinions, and to ask additional questions. This will help them comprehend the information in the story and gain confidence in their growing abilities.

Paragraph 1: When the family finally arrived in the United States, where did they land? *(West Coast)* Could they communicate easily? *(no; they spoke very little English)*

Paragraph 2: How did they feel? *(lost; depersonalized, frightened, alone)*

Paragraph 3: Who would help them in the United States? *(a community group in Maine)* Where would they live? *(in Maine)* (NOTE: You might introduce the word *sponsor* = person or group responsible for the support of (in this case) refugees immigrating to the United States [See Chapter 11 for **or**.])

Paragraph 4: What did the family see that they liked after they left Immigration? *(huge high-rises, stretches of highway, rushing people; peace, no gunfire, no threats)* What did they see that they didn't like? *(the way teenagers dressed and talked)*

Paragraph 5: How did the family travel across the United States? *(by plane and train)* What did they see? *(snow-capped Rockies, wheat fields of the Midwest, boats on the Mississippi, beauty of the Great Lakes; high-rises, interstate highways)*

Paragraph 6: (Explain: *Down East* = in or into Coastal Maine) What does *felt they were in heaven* mean? *(they were overwhelmed by the beauty of the scenery, breathed the sea breeze with pleasure)* Describe the Maine coast. *(See text.)*

Paragraph 7: What did the volunteer committee do? *(provided a place to live, clothing, household articles)* Does every refugee/immigrant family have such sponsors? *(no)*

Paragraph 8: What job did the committee find for Nari? *(sewing dresses and coats)* What job did the committee find for Yik Yam? *(helping in the fields; helping a fisherman)* What did the family do at night? *(studied English)*

Paragraph 9: Why didn't Yik Yam want to accept a loan? *(the family had always been independent)* Does he intend to pay off the loan? *(yes, as quickly as possible)*

Paragraph 10: Was the family completely happy or sad? *(neither; they had mixed feelings: sometimes happy, sometimes sad)*

Paragraph 11: Why did they feel nostalgia about their homeland? *(they would probably never see it again)*

Paragraph 12: At the end of this part of the family's odyssey, how does the future look for them? *(hopeful)* Explain why.

Chapter 8: The *ū* Sound

Tell students that in this lesson they will learn one letter combination that makes the *ū* sound (as in *union* and *cube*).

Page 110   Sound: ew = *ū* (*yew*)

Explain that the **ew** in *yew* sounds like the *ū* in *mule, union, cue,* etc. Say *yew* and point to it in the *Compare* section; it is different from *up, blue ($\overline{oo}$), wet, weep.*

Page 111   ## Sentences with the ew = $\bar{u}$ Sound

Call attention to the **WORD ALERT** section. Emphasize the differences between the words that follow the **ew** = $\bar{u}$ sound and spelling and the words in the **WORD ALERT**. Encourage students to find and circle the **WORD ALERT** exceptions in the sentences.

Page 113   ## Review: Phonetic Elements That Make Long-Vowel Sounds

Explain that this page provides a summary of all the combinations of letters that make long-vowel sounds:

1. Open syllables (Chapter 2);

2. Long vowels with silent **e** (Chapter 3);

3. Other letter combinations that make long-vowel sounds (Chapters 4–8).

Encourage students to use this page as a reference. You might suggest that they mark it with a paper clip.

Page 114   ## Review: Summary Chart of Words with Long-Vowel Sounds

Point out that the Summary Chart has one sample word for each of the five long-vowel sounds for each of the twenty common initial consonants (**x** is omitted).

Read across, starting with vowels alone. The object is to emphasize how the different vowels make the words sound different. On many of the lines, words are quite similar in other aspects to emphasize the vowel differences. Point out different consonant sounds: Line 3: soft **c** in both *cereal* and *cite*; Line 6: soft **g** in both *genius* and *giant*.

Encourage students to use this page as a reference. You might suggest that they mark it with a paper clip.

Unit Three: Special Sounds

Tell students that until now they have been reading long-vowel sounds in different spellings. Before that, they learned short-vowel sounds. Now they will learn a third category of vowel sounds—Special Sounds. These sounds are neither long nor short; they are entirely different.

Chapter 9: The $\overline{oo}$ Sound

Tell students that in this chapter they will learn five letter combinations that make the $\overline{oo}$ sound. They will also learn several exceptions in the **WORD ALERT** sections.

Page 125   ## Sentences with the ue = $\overline{oo}$ Sound

Call attention to the *WORD ALERT* section. Emphasize the differences between the words that follow the **ue** = $\overline{oo}$ sound and spelling and the words in the *WORD ALERT*. Encourage students to find and circle the *WORD ALERT* exceptions in the sentences.

    NOTE: Point out the *WORD ALERT* exceptions with the silent **ue**: *tongue, vague, vogue.*

Page 126   ## Sound: ui = $\overline{oo}$ (*fruit*)

Explain that the **ui** in *fruit* sounds like $\overline{oo}$ in *moon*, **ew** in *jewel*, etc. Say *fruit* and point to it in the *Compare* section; it is different from *foot, yew, cubic, sit.*

Page 127   ## Sentences with the ui = $\overline{oo}$ Sound

Call attention to the *WORD ALERT* section. Emphasize the differences between the words that follow the **ui** = $\overline{oo}$ sound and spelling and the words in the *WORD ALERT*. Encourage students to find and circle the *WORD ALERT* exceptions in the sentences.

Page 128   ## Sound: ou = $\overline{oo}$ (*soup*)

Explain that the **ou** in *soup* sounds like $\overline{oo}$ in *moon*, **ui** in *fruit*, etc. Say *soup* and point to it in the *Compare* section; it is different from *foot, cube, hope.*

Page 129   ## Sentences with the ou = $\overline{oo}$ Sound

Call attention to the *WORD ALERT* section. Emphasize the differences between the words that follow the **ou** = $\overline{oo}$ sound and spelling and the words in the *WORD ALERT*. Encourage students to find and circle the *WORD ALERT* exceptions in the sentences.

Chapter 10: Other Sounds with o

Tell students that in this chapter they will learn four letter combinations that make other sounds with **o**. They will also learn exceptions in the *WORD ALERT* sections.

Page 133   ## Sound: ow = *ow* (*cow*)

Explain that the **ow** in *cow* sounds like *brown*. Say *cow* and point to it in the *Compare* section; it is different from *snow, stop, post, boat, colt, note, toe.*

Page 135   ## Sound: ou = *ow* (*house*)

Explain that the **ou** in *house* sounds like **ow** in *cow*. Say *house* and point to it in the *Compare* section; it is different from *snow, boat, host, colt, hot, mule, up.*

Page 136   ## Sentences with the ou = *ow* Sound

Call attention to the *WORD ALERT* section. Emphasize the differences between the words that follow the **ou** = *ow* sound and spelling and the words in the *WORD ALERT*.

    Encourage students to find and circle the *WORD ALERT* exceptions in the sentences. Point out the silent letters **gh, b, h.** Tell students they will learn more about silent letters in Chapter 14.

Page 137	*WORD ALERT:* **Sometimes ou = ŭ** **(country)**

Page 138	## Sentences with the ou = ŭ Sound

Although a *WORD ALERT*, this two-page lesson follows the same format as other *Sound* and *Sentences* pages in the unit because of its many important examples.

Explain that the **ou** in *country* sounds like the *ŭ* in *up*. Say *country* and point to it in the *Compare* section; it is different from *house, home, snow, cow*.

Page 139	## Sound: oi = *oi (coin)*

Explain that this sounds like **oi** in *coin*. Say *coin* and point to it in the *Compare* section; it is different from *mouse, country, pie, fruit, hold, eight, rain*.

Page 141	## Sound: oy = *oi (boy)*

Explain that the **oy** in *boy* sounds like **oi** in *coin, boil*. Say *boy* and point to it in the *Compare* section; it is different from *cow, house, country, moon, boat, foot*.

Pages 144–145	## Special Skill: Previewing Key Words of Three or More Syllables from Story 5

NOTE: See page 130 of this manual for pronunciation of words with **ire**.

Additional Words from Story 5

Remind students that they have already learned most of these additional words. If possible, provide paper so that they can practice sounding out and writing the words. Ask volunteers to list them on the board.

1. ref u gee	refugee	12. ex pen sive	expensive
2. od ys sey	odyssey	13. in ves ti ga tion	investigation
3. fam i ly	family	14. con sid ered	considered
4. dif fer ent	different	15. ev ery one	everyone
5. ben e fit	benefit	16. beau ti ful	beautiful
6. con gest ed	congested	17. pro vid ed	provided
7. o ver come	overcome	18. ren o vate	renovate
8. in no va tive	innovative	19. de cid ed	decided
9. wel com ing	welcoming	20. won der ful	wonderful
10. com mit tee	committee	21. doc u ments	documents
11. cus tom ers	customers	22. se cu ri ty	security

Pages 146–149	## Story 5: A Refugee's Odyssey: Part 3: Real Estate

This story consolidates the skills taught in Chapters 7, 8, 9, and 10. (See "How to Use the *Stories*" on pages 122–124 of this manual and the phonetic specifications following the story in the text.)

Discussion Questions

Select from the following questions those that are appropriate for your class; ask other questions as well. Encourage students to respond, to give their answers and opinions, and to ask additional questions. This will help them comprehend the information in the story and gain confidence in their growing abilities.

Paragraph 1: What did Nari do to earn money? *(seamstress; independent businesswoman)* What machine had she learned to use? *(sewing machine)*

Paragraph 2: How were the children doing? *(enrolled in school, succeeding there; had friends, played in after-school games, members of Scouts, played musical instruments in the band)*

Paragraph 3: What was Yik Yam's job? *(assistant manager of a big discount chain)* What benefits did he receive? *(in-house management courses, night school)*

Paragraph 4: How did the children's English sound? *(like "native" Americans')* How did the parents speak English? *(with an accent)* How did they feel about idioms? *(sometimes they were stumped by them; some sounded very funny to them)* What was their attitude toward the future? *(they hoped and dreamed)*

Paragraph 5: (Explain: *dream* = a hopeful plan they want to come true; *equity* = money value in property above the mortgage owed; *nest egg* [idiom] = a sum of money saved for future use; *to leave* = in this case, an inheritance for their children) Why did Yik Yam and Nari want to own their own home? *(build equity, have a "nest egg"; leave something to their children)*

Paragraph 6: What did the Civil Rights Act of 1968 guarantee? *(that the Sok family could not be discriminated against in housing; they could buy any property they could afford)*

Paragraph 7: What is a real estate broker? *(a person who sells real estate)* a co-broker? *(a second broker participating in a real estate sale)* a condominium? *(part of a building owned by a private party)* a cooperative? *(an apartment that is a privately owned share in a building or complex with certain rights and obligations)*

Paragraph 8: What kind of home did the family decide to buy? *(a three-family house zoned for business)* What were the advantages? *(Nari could have her business; they could collect rent from two tenants)* (NOTE: You might want to introduce *financing* = mortgage, loan from a bank for buying a house.) (**or** will be taught in Chapter 11)

Paragraph 9: Was buying a house a simple or complex procedure? *(complex)*

Paragraph 10: (Explain: *legal advice, legal counsel* = advice from a lawyer [**aw** in Chapter 12])

Paragraph 11: How did they make their down payment? *(money they had saved for ten years)*

Paragraph 12: What are four kinds of common banking institutions that lend money for buying a home? *(credit union, savings and loan association, mutual savings bank, cooperative bank)* Why did Yik Yam and Nari choose the credit union? *(they had their savings account at the credit union; the credit union had loaned them money before; the credit union gave them the lowest interest rate)*

Paragraph 13: What does *title* refer to? *(ownership)* Why did the credit union have to check the title? *(to find out about liens, easements, encroachments, other encumbrances)* What is an appraisal? *(evaluation)*

Paragraph 14: What is *escrow?* (money kept by a third party—often a bank—until some condition has been fulfilled) What is *closing?* (the time when the property changes hands)

Paragraph 15: What is a deed? (document that says who owns something) What does *foreclose* mean? (to take back something that has not been paid for)

Paragraphs 16–17: Describe the location of the house. (See text.)

Paragraphs 18–19: Describe the grounds around the house. (See text.)

Paragraphs 20–21: Describe the overall condition of the outside of the house. (See text.)

Paragraph 22: Describe the inside of the house. Did it need repair? (See text.)

Paragraph 23: Was the family willing to repair the inside of the house? (yes)

Paragraph 24: What part of the house would they occupy? (the ground-floor unit) What would they use the front room for? (Nari's business) What is a *legitimate business expense?* (cost and upkeep of space needed for business)

Paragraph 25: What does Yik Yam think of the United States? (wonderful country)

Chapter 11: *r*-Related Vowel Sounds

Tell students that in this chapter they will learn twelve letter combinations of **r**-related vowel sounds. They will also learn exceptions in the **WORD ALERT** sections.

Page 152   Sound: or = *or (corn)*

Explain that the **or** in *corn* sounds like the sight words *or* and *for.* Say *corn* and point to it in the *Compare* section; it is different from *boy, coin, cow, house, moon, soup, old.*

Page 153   Sentences with the or = *or* Sound

Call attention to the **WORD ALERT** section. Emphasize the differences between the words that follow the **or** = *or* sound and spelling and the words in the **WORD ALERT.** Encourage students to find and circle the **WORD ALERT** exceptions in the sentences.

Page 154   Sound: er = *er (computer)*

Explain that the **er** in *computer* sounds like *were.* Say *computer* and point to it in the *Compare* section; it is different from *corn, or, jewel, few, blue, feet.*

Page 156   Sound: ir = *er (bird)*

Explain that the **ir** in *bird* sounds like **er** in *runner, her,* etc. Say *bird* and point to it in the *Compare* section; it is different from *piece, horn, fruit, pie, child.*

Page 157   Sentences with the ir = *er* Sound

Call attention to the **WORD ALERT** section. Emphasize the differences between the words that follow the **ir** = *er* sound and spelling and the word in the **WORD ALERT.**

Page 158 Sound: ur = *er (nurse)*

Explain that the **ur** in *nurse* sounds like **er** in *computer,* **ir** in *bird,* etc. Say *nurse* and point to it in the *Compare* section; it is different from *corn, soup, blue, suit, mouse.*

Page 159 Sentences with the ur = *er* Sound

Call attention to the *WORD ALERT* section. Emphasize the differences between the words that follow the **ur** = *er* sound and spelling and the words in the *WORD ALERT.*

Page 160 Sound: ear = *er (pearl)*

Explain that the **ear** in *pearl* sounds like **er** in *runner,* **ur** in *nurse,* etc. Say *pearl* and point to it in the *Compare* section; it is different from *corn, few, meat, bread, they.*

Page 161 Sentences with the ear = *er* Sound

Call attention to the *WORD ALERT* section. Emphasize the differences between the words that follow the **ear** = *er* sound and spelling and the words in the *WORD ALERT.* Encourage students to find and circle the *WORD ALERT* exceptions in the sentences.

Page 162 Sound: our = *er (journal)*

Explain that the **our** in *journal* sounds like **er** in *computer,* **ir** in *bird,* etc. Say *journal* and point to it in the *Compare* section; it is different from *house, you, corn, boy.*

Page 163 Sentences with the our = *er* Sound

Call attention to the *WORD ALERT* section. Emphasize the differences between the words that follow the **our** = *er* sound and spelling and the words in the *WORD ALERT.*

Page 164 Sound: wor = *wer (worm)*

Explain that the **wor** in *worm* sounds like **er** in *were, her, swerve,* etc. Say *worm* and point to it in the *Compare* section; it is different from *wobble, work, wood.*

Page 166 Sound: ar = *ar (car)*

Explain that the **ar** in *car* sounds like *are.* Say *car* and point to it in the *Compare* section; it is different from *pearl, carrot, rain, hay.*

Page 167 Sentences with the ar = *ar* Sound

Call attention to the *WORD ALERT* section. Emphasize the differences between the words that follow the **ar** = *ar* sound and spelling and the words in the *WORD ALERT.* Encourage students to find and circle the *WORD ALERT* exceptions in the sentences.

Page 168 Sound: air = *air (chair)*

Explain that this sounds like the **air** in *chair.* Say *chair* and point to it in the *Compare* section; it is different from *car, pearl, pain, pine, pat, rain.*

Page 169 ## Sentences with the air = *air* Sound

Call attention to the **WORD ALERT** section. Emphasize the differences between the words that follow the **air** = *air* sound and spelling and the words in the **WORD ALERT**. Encourage students to find and circle the **WORD ALERT** exceptions in the sentences.

Page 170 ## Sound: are = *air (square)*

Explain that the **are** in *square* sounds like the **air** in *chair, hair,* etc. Say *square* and point to it in the *Compare* section; it is different from *car, they are, computer, pearl, rain, cape.*

Page 171 ## Sentences with the are = *air* Sound

Call attention to the **WORD ALERT** section. Emphasize the differences between the words that follow the **are** = *air* sound and spelling and the word in the **WORD ALERT**. Encourage students to find and circle the **WORD ALERT** in the sentences.

Page 172 ## Sound: ary = *airy (dictionary)*

Explain that the **ary** in *dictionary* sounds like **airy** in *hairy, dairy,* etc. Say *dictionary* and point to it in the *Compare* section; it is different from *art, play, pearl, rain, marry.*

Page 174 ## Sound: ear = *air (bear)*

Explain that the **ear** in *bear* sounds like the **air** in *hair,* **are** in *hare,* etc. Say *bear* and point to it in the *Compare* section; it is different from *hear, bread, great.*

Page 175 ## Sentences with the ear = *air* Sound

Call attention to the **WORD ALERT** section. Emphasize the differences between the words that follow the **ear** = *air* sound and spelling and the word in the **WORD ALERT**. Encourage students to find and circle the **WORD ALERT** in the sentences.

Chapter 12: aw and Related Sounds

Tell students that in this chapter they will learn seven letter combinations with **a** that make **aw**-related vowel sounds. They will also learn exceptions in the **WORD ALERT** sections.

Page 180 ## Sound: aw = *aw (saw)*

Explain that this sounds like the **aw** in *saw*. Say *saw* and point to it in the *Compare* section; it is different from *car, chair, hay, rain, cable, paste.*

Page 181 ## Sentences with the aw = *aw* Sound

Call attention to the **WORD ALERT** section. Emphasize the differences between the words that follow the **aw** = *aw* sound and spelling and the words in the **WORD ALERT**. Encourage students to find and circle the **WORD ALERT** exceptions in the sentences.

Page 182 Sound: au = *aw (saucer)*

Explain that the **au** in *saucer* sounds like the **aw** in *saw, draw*, etc. Say *saucer* and point to it in the *Compare* section; it is different from *car, chair, fur, pay, rain*.

Page 183 Sentences with the au = *aw* Sound

Call attention to the **WORD ALERT** section. Emphasize the differences between the words that follow the **au** = *aw* sound and spelling and the words in the **WORD ALERT**. Encourage students to find and circle the **WORD ALERT** exceptions in the sentences.

Page 184 Sound: all = *awl (ball)*

Explain that the **all** in *ball* sound like the **aw** in *saw*, **au** in *saucer*, etc. Say *ball* and point to it in the *Compare* section; it is different from *car, angel, pal, hay, sail, stale*.

Page 186 Sound: al = *awl (salt)*

Explain that the **al** in *salt* sounds like the **all** in *ball*, **au** in *saucer*, **aw** in *saw*, etc. Say *salt* and point to it in the *Compare* section; it is different from *pal, Allen, tale, pain*.

Page 187 Sentences with the al = *awl* Sound

Call attention to the **WORD ALERT** section. Emphasize the differences between the words that follow the **al** = *awl* sound and spelling and the word in the **WORD ALERT**. Point out that the **WORD ALERT** *although* has a silent **gh**.

NOTE: Call attention to sentence #5. Read the sentence and point out that the word *salad* has the *ăl* sound they learned in Books One and Two, not the *aw* sound they are now learning.

Page 188 Sound: alk (silent l) = *awk (chalk)*

Explain that the **alk** in *chalk* sounds like the **awk** in *awkward, gawk*, **aw** in *saw*, etc. Point out that the **l** is a silent letter and that all the words below have the silent **l**. Say *chalk* and point to it in the *Compare* section; it is different from *talc, Hal, tale, ball* (where you can hear the **l**).

Page 189 Sentences with alk = *awk* Sound

Remind students that all of the words in the box have the silent **l**.

NOTE: In the first sentence, point out the male name *Hal*, noting that it has the *ăl* sound. Contrast *Hal* with the **alk** sound in *Walker*.

Page 190 Sound: qua = *quaw (quarter)*

Explain that the **qua** in *quarter* sounds like the **aw** in *saw*, **au** in *saucer*, etc. Say *quarter* and point to it in the *Compare* section; it is different from *quake, quack*.

Page 191 Sentences with the qua = *quaw* Sound

Remind students that in English, **q** is always followed by **u**.

> **Note**
>
> Since *quarter* is the featured word in this lesson, you may want to consider using this as an opportunity to talk about U.S. money. Your students might be interested in knowing that George Washington's profile is on the front of the quarter, and the bald eagle (the national bird of the United States—symbolizing freedom and power) decorates the back. If possible, have students look at a quarter. Tell them that it is also called twenty-five cents.
>
> Point out that they can now read most of the words on the quarter: LIBERTY; IN GOD WE TRUST; 19—; UNITED STATES OF AMERICA; QUARTER; DOLLAR. Over the eagle is E PLURIBUS UNUM—a Latin phrase meaning OUT OF MANY, ONE. This refers to the creation of the United States out of the original thirteen colonies. Since 1873, the law requires that this motto appear on one side of every U.S. coin.

Page 192   ## Sound: war = *wor (warm)*

Explain that the **war** in *warm* sounds like the **(w)or** in *worn*, **aw** in *saw*, etc. Say *warm* and point to it in the *Compare* section; it is different from *want, ware*.

Page 194   ## *WORD ALERT:* Sometimes wa = *wah (swan)*

Page 195   ## Sentences with the wa = *wah* Sound

Although a *WORD ALERT,* this two-page lesson follows the same format as other *Sound* and *Sentences* pages in the unit because of its many important examples. Explain that **wa** usually sounds like *was*, a sight word that they already know, and like **wa** in *swan, wasp,* and *swat* (see *Compare* line). It sounds different from **wa** (**wă**) in *wagon* and *wax*, from **wa** (**wā**) in *wave*, and from **aw** in *saw, saucer, ball,* and *quarter*. Say *swan* and point to it in the *Compare* section.

Page 196   ## *WORD ALERT:* Sometimes qua = *quah (squash)*

Explain that **qua** frequently sounds like *quah* as in *squash, quad,* and *qualify*. It sounds different from *quaw (quarter)* and from **quă** *(quack)* and from **quā** *(quake)*. Say *squash* and point it out in the *Compare* section.

Chapter 13: Special Consonant Sounds

The format of this chapter is somewhat different. Students will *Read, Write,* and *Listen and write* words that are exceptions to the rules. Have them concentrate on the new sounds.

Explain that in this chapter students will learn some new spellings that make the consonant sounds **f, sh, zh, k,** and **ch.** Encourage them to listen very carefully to hear the differences in sounds.

Emphasize the special sound in each of these lessons:

Page 200   **ph** = *f* not **p** = *pot* or **h** = *hot,* but *f* = *phone*

Page 201   **gh** = *f* not **g** = *got* or **h** = *hog,* but *f* = *cough*

Page 202   **ci** = *sh* not **ci** = *city,* but *sh* = *electrician* (as in *shelf, she,* and *glacier*)

Page 203   **su** = *sh* not **s** = *sun,* but *sh* = *sugar* (as in *shelf* and *she*); (**su** has a **zh** sound in *leisure* and *treasure*)

sion = *shun* not **si** = *sit*, but *shun* = *mansion;*

sion = *zhun (sometimes)* not **si** = *sit*, but *zhun* = *television **(WORD ALERT)**;*

tion = *shun* not **ti** = *tip*, but *shun* = *communication, station, education*

Page 205   ch = *k* not **ch** = *chest*, but *k* = *school* (as in *cake*);

tu = *ch* not **tu** = *tub*, but *ch* = *picture*

Page 207–208 ## Special Skill: Previewing Key Words of Three or More Syllables from Story 6

NOTE: See page 130 of this manual for pronunciation of words with **ire.**

Additional Words from Story 6

Remind students that they have already learned most of these additional words. If possible, provide paper so that they can practice sounding out and writing the words. Ask volunteers to list them on the board.

1. in clud ing   including
2. re plac ing   replacing
3. an y thing   anything
4. fre quent ly   frequently
5. how ev er   however
6. ser vi ces   services
7. ex pen sive   expensive

Pages 209—212 ## Story 6: Auto Maintenance

This story consolidates the skills taught in Chapters 11, 12, and 13. (See "How to Use the *Stories*" on pages 122–124 of this manual and the phonetic specifications following the story in the text.)

Discussion Questions

Select from the following questions those that are appropriate for your class; ask other questions as well. Encourage students to respond, to give their answers and opinions, and to ask additional questions. This will help them comprehend the information in the story and gain confidence in their growing abilities.

Paragraph 1: (Explain: *driving you up a wall* [Idiom, page 199]) What do Tyrone Parker and Walter Cooper do? *(co-own and operate an automobile repair shop and gas station)* What's the name of their garage? *(Auto Repairs, Inc.)* What services does their garage provide? *(diagnosis; repair and maintenance; towing)* (NOTE: Remind students that *Inc.* is the abbreviation for *Incorporated.*)

Paragraph 2: What is their "routine maintenance check"? *(See page 209.)*

Paragraphs 3 and 4: How many points are there on their checklist? *(thirty)* What do they check for? *(See text.)* What does *viscosity* mean? *(thickness)*

Paragraph 5: What is carbon monoxide? *(a colorless, odorless, toxic gas)* What are exhaust emissions? *(gases that the car's exhaust system emits)*

Paragraph 6: What can Walter and Tyrone repair? *(catalytic converters and engines)* What are some kinds of fuel that vehicles use? *(leaded or unleaded gas, diesel fuel, gasoline-ethanol blends)*

Paragraph 7: What don't they like to do? *(care for the exterior and interior appearance of vehicles)* To whom do they refer this kind of work? *(to their friend, Pauline Hawkins, who owns Caring for Cars, Inc.)*

Paragraphs 8 and 9: What do the employees of Caring for Cars, Inc. do? *(See text.)* What luxury touches does Pauline Hawkins provide? *(AM-FM stereo radios with electronic tuners and cassette tape players; roof carriers, ski racks, anti-theft devices)* How do you get a discount from Pauline? *(mention that Tyrone or Walter sent you)*

Paragraph 10: What is a master mechanic? an automotive specialist? a finishing specialist? Are Walter Cooper and Tyrone Parker cooperative? thrifty? fair?

Chapter 14: Silent Letters

The format of this chapter, as shown on page 214, is somewhat different. Students will *Read, Write,* and *Listen and write* words that have silent letters. Have them concentrate on the words with these silent letters. Sentences are offered on the *Review, Bonus,* and *Story* pages.

The words are presented in three columns:

Column 1: words with the featured silent letters (**k, w, b, gh, h, g, s, t, l, p**);

Column 2: words that they sound like (there are no silent letters in these words);

Column 3: words that they sound different from (where the featured letter is pronounced).

Explain that in this chapter, students will learn words in which letters are silent; for example, **k** in *knife,* **w** in *wrench,* **b** in *comb,* **gh** in *light,* **h** in *hour,* **g** in *sign,* **s** in *island,* **t** in *whistle,* **l** in *palm,* and **p** in *receipt.* Point out that these letters say nothing. Encourage students to listen very carefully to hear the differences in sounds. (Compare and contrast sound vs. no sound: for example, *kite* vs. *knife.*) Reassure students that they will learn one silent letter (or two, in the case of **gh**) at a time, and that they already know some of the words.

Page 214 ## Silent k (kn = n) (knife)

Explain that in the first column, the letter **k** is silent, as in *knife.* The **k** doesn't say anything. The beginning of the word sounds like *nine.* The **k** doesn't sound like *kite.* Compare and contrast the three columns of words with students.

Page 215 ## Silent w (wr = r) (wrench)

Explain that in the first column, the letter **w** is silent, as in *wrench.* The **w** doesn't say anything. Compare and contrast the three columns of words with students.

Page 216 ## Silent b (comb)

Explain that in the first column, the letter **b** is silent, as in *comb.* The **b** doesn't say anything. Compare and contrast the three columns of words with students.

Pages 217–218 ## Silent gh (light)

Explain that in the first column, the letters **gh** are silent, as in *light.* The letters **gh** don't say anything. Compare and contrast the three columns of words with students.

Page 219 ## Silent h (hour)

Explain that in the first column, the letter **h** is silent, as in *hour.* The **h** doesn't say anything. Compare and contrast the three columns of words with students.

Silent g *(sign)* and Silent s *(island)*

Explain that in the first column, the letter **g** is silent, as in *sign*. The **g** doesn't say anything. Compare and contrast the three columns of words with students.

Explain that in the first column, the letter **s** is silent, as in *island*. The **s** doesn't say anything. Compare and contrast the three columns of words with students.

Silent t *(whistle)*

Explain that in the first column, the letter **t** is silent, as in *whistle*. The **t** doesn't say anything. Compare and contrast the three columns of words with students.

Silent l *(palm)*

Explain that in the first column, the letter **l** is silent, as in *palm*. The **l** doesn't say anything. Compare and contrast the three columns of words with students.

Silent p *(receipt)*

Explain that in the first column, the letter **p** is silent, as in *receipt*. The **p** doesn't say anything. Compare and contrast the three columns of words with students.

Chapter 15: Contractions and Word Endings with Long-Vowel Roots

This chapter offers summary charts of the language skills students have learned. Each lesson has a different format. The lessons can be used in many ways: *Read, Write, Listen and write, Compare,* and *Discuss.*

Focus on the featured skill in each lesson.

Summary: Contractions

Emphasize the vowel sound in each contraction.

Summary: Adding ing, ed, and er Endings to Long-Vowel Words

Emphasize the vowel sound. Point out:

1. "Long" vowel sound "doesn't need any help." **Don't** double the consonant before endings.

2. "Short" vowel sound "does need help." **Do** double the consonant before endings.

Summary: Pronunciation of ed Past Tense in Verbs with Long Vowels and Special Vowel Sounds

Emphasize that **ed** endings have three different sounds. Explain that these endings fall into groups depending on the ending sound of the root word.

Tell students that they don't have to learn what these root word ending sounds are, but that they need to read them and be aware of the reasons for the different sounds of **ed.**

Pages 231–232   ## Special Skill: Previewing Key Words of Three or More Syllables from Story 7

NOTE: See page 130 of this manual for pronunciation of words with **ire.**

Additional Words from Story 7

Remind students that they have already learned most of these additional words. If possible, provide paper so that they can practice sounding out and writing the words. Ask volunteers to list them on the board.

1.	an y way	anyway	19.	Sat ur day	Saturday
2.	ac cept ed	accepted	20.	ev ery thing	everything
3.	com pa ny	company	21.	ac ces si ble	accessible
4.	sud den ly	suddenly	22.	qual i ty	quality
5.	sym pa thet ic	sympathetic	23.	ac com pa ny	accompany
6.	sal a ry	salary	24.	re spon si ble	responsible
7.	A mer i can	American	25.	ter rif ic	terrific
8.	ex cel lent	excellent	26.	re solv ing	resolving
9.	com pe tent	competent	27.	in struc tions	instructions
10.	grad u at ed	graduated	28.	com pu ter	computer
11.	com mu ni ty	community	29.	pos i tive	positive
12.	u ni ver si ty	university	30.	em ploy ee	employee
13.	cam pus es	campuses	31.	de ter mined	determined
14.	em ploy er	employer	32.	sen si tive	sensitive
15.	Bach e lor's	Bachelor's	33.	ex per i ence	experience
16.	in de pen dent	independent	34.	a vail a ble	available
17.	neigh bor hood	neighborhood	35.	op por tu ni ty	opportunity
18.	in ter est ed	interested	36.	croc o dile	crocodile

Pages 233–237   ## Story 7: Patricia Knowlton's Job-Hunting Campaign

This story consolidates the skills taught in Chapters 14 and 15. (See "How to Use the *Stories*" on pages 122–124 of this manual and the phonetic specifications following the story in the text.)

Discussion Questions

Select from the following questions those that are appropriate for your class; ask other questions as well. Encourage students to respond, to give their answers and opinions, and to ask additional questions. This will help them comprehend the information in the story and gain confidence in their growing abilities.

Paragraph 1: How does Patricia feel? (What was her attitude)? *(blue, down in the dumps)* Why? *(didn't get the job; no day-care available)*

Paragraph 2: What did the letter of rejection say? *(the company found an applicant whose background was preferable)*

Paragraph 3: What does Patricia decide to do? *(be more positive; "knock them for a loop")*

Paragraph 4: Is her son, John, loving and supportive? *(yes)*

Paragraph 5: Why is Patricia upset? *(She wanted a reasonably good job for a respectable salary.)*

Paragraph 6: How does her résumé describe her? *(schooling, work experience)*

Paragraph 7: How would people who know Patricia describe her? *(single mother of two; 37 years old, 5 feet 8 inches tall, weighs close to 150 pounds; strong, handsome, bright, independent, determined; courteous, dependable)* What does an employer want to know? *(person's work credentials, education, character references)* What personal information is private and doesn't need to be disclosed to an employer, according to the law? *(a person's looks, weight, height, age, marital status)*

Paragraph 8: What section of the newspaper does Patricia use to look for a job? *(the classified ads, Help Wanted ads)*

Paragraphs 9–10: What is the ad for? *(supervisor of a computer room)* What duties will be required to be performed? *(supervising and training staff; ensuring that systems operate every day; writing memos and quarterly reports; making monthly presentations to management)*

Paragraph 11: What qualifications are needed? *(strong analytical skills; able to work under pressure)*

Paragraph 12: What is the name of the company? *(Quantum Leap)* What benefits does the company offer? *(medical, dental, life insurance; profit sharing; tuition reimbursement; day care)*

Paragraph 13: If Patricia wants to apply for the job, what must she do? *(send résumé and cover letter)*

Paragraph 14: Explain the following terms: *affirmative action, equal opportunity employer, handicapped accessible.*

Paragraph 15: How does Patricia write her cover letter? *(on scrap paper; four rough drafts; typed it on good quality paper)* What is a résumé? *(a summary of one's qualifications and work experience)*

(NOTE: Point out that *résumé* and *resume* are different words: *résumé* is a French word that means summarized; to write a brief history of one's qualifications and work experience. [Call attention to the accent marks above the two **e**'s, and tell students that these provide the clue that the word is not English.] *Resume* means to start again [some activity that you had been doing]. It is also correct to write *résumé* without the accent marks in English: *resume* or *resumé.*)

Paragraphs 16–24: What are the parts of a letter?

> **Note**
> You may want to discuss the parts of a letter with students. Use the letter in the story as a model:
>
> 1. **Letterhead** (the printed or engraved name and address at the top of customized stationery; companies use this)
> 2. **Heading** (the return address of the person who is writing the letter, and the date)

3. **Inside address** (the name and address of the person to whom the letter is written)

4. **Salutation** (*Dear* + the name of the person to whom the letter is written; otherwise, *Dear Sir/Madam:*)

5. **Body of letter** (this begins with an introductory paragraph, explaining the purpose of the letter)

6. **Complimentary close** (*Sincerely, Sincerely yours,* or something similar)

7. **Signature** (the sender's name, handwritten, with name typed beneath it)

Paragraph 19: What does Patricia do in the first paragraph of her letter? *(tells the purpose of the letter)*

Paragraph 20: What does she describe in the second paragraph? *(experience, education, other qualifications she wants to emphasize)*

Paragraph 21: Explain that this is a summary paragraph that states Patricia's ability and willingness to work with the equipment and the other employees.

Paragraph 22: What is Patricia asking for? *(an appointment to meet and talk about the job in more detail)*

Paragraph 23: Point out that simple closings are more effective. Note that a comma follows the complimentary close.

Paragraph 24: Patricia will sign her name above where it's typed. Why do many people both type and sign their names? *(some people's signatures are hard to read)*

Paragraph 25: How did Patricia feel after Ms. Carlisle called her? *(very happy; excited)*

Paragraph 26: How did she prepare for the interview? *(she went over in her mind how she would speak and act.)*

Paragraph 27: What did she have in her briefcase? *(a ballpoint pen, a small notebook; a list of references)* What did she wear? *(a white blouse, a navy blue suit; pearl and gold necklace)* Did her children think she looked good? *(yes)* Do you? Do you think Patricia will get the job? Why or why not?

NOTE: Explain that this story contains actual samples of a résumé and a cover letter, as well as samples of a rejection letter and a newspaper job ad (Help Wanted ad).

Additional Activities

1. Have students copy the résumé and/or the cover letter. They can change the information if they want.

2. Encourage students to write their own résumé, based on the model. If appropriate for your students, point out that a homemaker and a business executive share the same skills: each can *organize, prepare, present, teach, supervise, create, direct, problem-solve, initiate,* and *be efficient* and *cost effective.* Every student in the class can prepare a résumé based on personal talents, abilities, and experience.

3. Use the job ads in the local newspaper as material for a discussion about skills employers are looking for, benefits offered, potential for future growth. Help students decode any abbreviations.

4. Students can practice answering job ads. Check to see that they have responded to the items listed by potential employers.

Note

The U.S. Department of Labor, Bureau of Labor Statistics publishes two valuable career guides that are available in most public libraries:

1. *Occupational Outlook Handbook*—tells about different kinds of jobs and the qualifications needed to apply for them. (This book is also published by National Textbook Company.)

2. *Exploring Careers*, "The World of Work and You"—explores different kinds of careers from a more personal perspective and asks questions that help people decide what may be appropriate for them, based on their lifestyles.

Both documents contain photographs of real people (male/female; multicultural; all ages; all abilities) doing different kinds of work in different settings. The presentation in both books is informative, positive, and up to date (revised often).

Appendices

There are six appendices, each with its own format. The skills summarized in them appear throughout Book Three. The material in the appendices can be used in a variety of ways:

1. To provide review material for students at the end of Book Three.

2. To provide reinforcement of the skills learned, and to show students how far they have advanced. (Note how many names, places, proverbs, idioms, and so on that students can read and understand.)

3. To provide material to

   • generate sentences for *Listen and write*

   • offer additional practice

   • use as reference charts

Refer to the appendices as needed throughout the book.

Appendix A: Names

Provides a list of commonly used first (male and female) and last names for every letter of the English alphabet using long vowels and special sounds.

Appendix B: Proverbs

All the proverbs presented in Book Three are summarized in this appendix. The list tells in which chapters the phonetic elements in the proverbs are presented. (Note: The proverb itself is presented on the *Bonus* page with the highest chapter number. For example, the first proverb on page 239 uses elements taught in Chapters 3, 5, and 11, and is presented on the *Bonus* page of Chapter 11.)

Appendix C: Geography

Provides the names of major geographical areas using long vowels and special sounds: continents, countries, cities, and the fifty states of the United States.

Appendix D: Homonyms

Do not expect your students to master this list. It merely anticipates their growing powers of observation and awareness that different words can sound the same. Emphasize that although these words sound the same, they have entirely different spellings and meanings.

If appropriate for your class, work with students to create sentences that illustrate the correct usage of the homonyms. For example:

1. This set of dishes includes eight *bowls* for soup or rice.

2. Our company *bowl*ing team just won the championship!

3. *Boll* weevils are small beetles that destroy the *boll* of the cotton plants.

4. The word *bole* refers to the trunk of a tree.

Appendix E: Foreign Words in Common English Usage

Explain that these foreign words are commonly used by English speakers. Point out that they don't follow all the phonetic rules taught in Book Three because they are from other languages. Treat the words as sight words; encourage students to memorize them.

Appendix F: Major Sounds of the Consonants and Vowels

This appendix provides both a review and a summary of all the different sounds that one letter or combination of letters can make in English.

When students are sounding out a word, they can try one pronunciation. If that doesn't seem right, they can try another. For example, when students see **ou,** they can say *ō* (as in *though*), *o͞o* (as in *soup*), *o͝o* (as in *would*), *ow* (as in *house*) *aw* (as in *ought*), or *ŭ* (as in *country*).

About the Authors

Judith S. Rubenstein received a Doctorate in Education from Harvard University and a B.A. in French from Wellesley College. Dr. Rubenstein has taught English language skills abroad and in Massachusetts (Harvard University Extension School, adult education programs, and private practice). She has published articles on various subjects in *The Boston Globe, The Journal of the American Medical Association, Adolescence,* and *Nature,* as well as having written, edited, and translated English and foreign language materials. As an educational consultant, Dr. Rubenstein is committed to teaching adults and children how to communicate effectively on many levels. Currently, she is creating a wide range of learning materials for speakers of English and other languages.

Janet M. Gubbay received a B.S. in sociology and anthropology from Northeastern University and studied counseling at the Northeastern Graduate School of Education. She is an experienced project leader, researcher, writer, editor, and book designer. As a writer and editor, she is committed to creating learning materials that promote personal growth and enrichment for people of all ages and backgrounds. Currently, she is writing books for children that focus on building self-esteem and encouraging independence of thought.

NTC ESL/EFL TEXTS AND MATERIAL
Junior High—Adult Education

Computer Software
Amigo
Basic Vocabulary Builder on Computer

Language and Culture Readers
Beginner's English Reader
Advanced Beginner's English Reader
Cultural Encounters in the U.S.A.
Passport to America Series
  California Discovery
  Adventures in the Southwest
  The Coast-to-Coast Mystery
  The New York Connection
Discover America Series
  California, Chicago, Florida, Hawaii,
  New England, New York, Texas,
  Washington, D.C.
Looking at America Series
  Looking at American Signs, Looking at
  American Food, Looking at American
  Recreation, Looking at American Holidays
Time: We the People
Communicative American English
English á la Cartoon

Text/Audiocassette Learning Packages
Speak Up! Sing Out!
Listen and Say It Right in English!

Transparencies
Everyday Situations in English

Duplicating Masters and
Black-line Masters
The Complete ESL/EFL Cooperative and
  Communicative Activity Book
Easy Vocabulary Games
Vocabulary Games
Advanced Vocabulary Games
Play and Practice!
Basic Vocabulary Builder
Practical Vocabulary Builder
Beginning Activities for English
  Language Learners
Intermediate Activities for English
  Language Learners
Advanced Activities for English
  Language Learners

Language-Skills Texts
Starting English with a Smile
English with a Smile
More English with a Smile
English Survival Series
  Building Vocabulary, Recognizing Details,
  Identifying Main Ideas, Writing Sentences
  and Paragraphs, Using the Context
English Across the Curriculum
Essentials of Reading and Writing English
Everyday English
Everyday Situations for Communicating in
  English
Learning to Listen in English
Listening to Communicate in English
Communication Skillbooks
Living in the U.S.A.
Basic English Vocabulary Builder Activity Book
Basic Everyday Spelling Workbook
Practical Everyday Spelling Workbook

Advanced Readings and Communicative
  Activities for Oral Proficiency
Practical English Writing Skills
Express Yourself in Written English
Campus English
English Communication Skills for Professionals
Speak English!
Read English!
Write English!
Orientation in American English
Building English Sentences
Grammar for Use
Grammar Step-by-Step
Listening by Doing
Reading by Doing
Speaking by Doing
Vocabulary by Doing
Writing by Doing
Look, Think and Write

Life- and Work-Skills Texts
English for Success
Building Real Life English Skills
Everyday Consumer English
Book of Forms
Essential Life Skills series
Finding a Job in the United States
English for Adult Living
Living in English
Prevocational English

TOEFL and University Preparation
NTC's Preparation Course for the TOEFL®
NTC's Practice Tests for the TOEFL®
How to Apply to American Colleges
  and Universities
The International Student's Guide
  to the American University

Dictionaries and References
ABC's of Languages and Linguistics
Everyday American English Dictionary
Building Dictionary Skills in
  English (workbook)
Beginner's Dictionary of American
  English Usage
Beginner's English Dictionary
  Workbook
NTC's American Idioms Dictionary
NTC's Dictionary of American Slang
  and Colloquial Expressions
NTC's Dictionary of Phrasal Verbs
NTC's Dictionary of Grammar Terminology
Essential American Idioms
Contemporary American Slang
Forbidden American English
101 American English Idioms
101 American English Proverbs
Practical Idioms
Essentials of English Grammar
The Complete ESL/EFL Resource Book
Safari Grammar
Safari Punctuation
303 Dumb Spelling Mistakes
TESOL Professional Anthologies
  Grammar and Composition
  Listening, Speaking, and Reading
  Culture

For further information or a current catalog, write:
National Textbook Company
a division of *NTC Publishing Group*
4255 West Touhy Avenue
Lincolnwood, Illinois 60646-1975 U.S.A.